CW00519832

The Cases That India Forgot

Praise for the Book

'This book narrates ten captivating stories about India's "forgotten" cases. Chandrachud's writing is simple for the lay reader and yet holds the attention of both the lawyer and the legal scholar. The book ignites interest in the law and in our Constitution, and is also a must-read for those who are in the legal profession. Chandrachud's book is eminently readable. You will enjoy it thoroughly.'

Zia Mody

'Stories, well-told, are more readable than judgements of courts. And this is a book of stories about select cases, written in a style that would have pleased the great master of law and language, Lord Denning. It is a must-read. Once you read them you will never forget them.'

Fali Nariman

'The Supreme Court of India has come to occupy centre space in public discourse and consciousness. This puts the Court in the unenviable position of being the cynosure of public attention – and concomitant public scrutiny. An exposition of the setting and context in which important cases were decided would help the informed lay opinion maker demystify the Court. The author has wisely chosen issues of contemporary relevance which were addressed in *forgotten* cases and presented them in a style that identifies the strengths but also spots the moments of weakness of the institution. A must-read for those interested in understanding the working of our powerful Court.'

Harish Salve

'There's nothing more riveting than the well-told account of a complex court case, where intriguing arguments collide with each other whilst the fate of real people hangs precariously in the balance. That's what makes this collection of stories irresistible. If you are a fan of Perry Mason or *Rumpole of the Bailey*, these real-life accounts will take you to the next level – the intriguing twists and turns that often occur in the defence of our Constitution.'

Karan Thapar

The Cases That India Forgot

Chintan Chandrachud

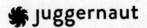

JUGGERNAUT BOOKS
KS House, 118 Shahpur Jat, New Delhi 110049, India

First published by Juggernaut Books 2019

10 9 8 7 6 5 4 3 2 1

P-ISBN: 9789353450823
E-ISBN: 9789353450830

Typeset in Adobe Caslon Pro by R. Ajith Kumar, Noida

Printed at Replika Press Pvt. Ltd

'If I have seen further,
it is by standing upon the shoulders of giants.'

Isaac Newton

With deep gratitude to
Prabha and Ajju
Nani and Baba

Contents

Contents

Part 4: National Security

Preface

A few years ago, I began writing op-eds for newspapers with a view to engaging with those outside my profession. One of the early comments that I received was that my writing was still somewhat 'legalistic' and difficult to access for those with little or no training in law. This turned out to be a wider complaint against lawyers and legal scholars – that their writing was often hard to read and difficult to understand. The vast majority of writing by lawyers (including commentary which is directed towards the general public) is remarkably inaccessible, although this is gradually changing with time. Addressing this complaint was the primary impetus behind the book.

The Supreme Court and high courts are at the epicentre of public life in India. Almost every political, economic, religious and historical question is (rightly or wrongly) formulated as a legal or constitutional question

and arises for judicial decision. Some of the cases that
the Supreme Court and high courts decide are etched
in public memory because of their social significance
or political impact. The Mandal Commission case set
the benchmark for determining who the beneficiaries
of reservation could be, while the Kesavananda case
imposed limitations on Parliament's authority to amend
the Constitution. Entire volumes are dedicated to these
cases, which have been analysed and dissected threadbare.

For each of these landmark cases, however, there is
a catalogue of cases that is not in the general public
consciousness – or at any rate, no longer in the public
consciousness if it once was. Each chapter of this book
focuses on one of these 'forgotten' cases – cases that are
not in the public memory, but should be. The cases are
divided into four overarching themes – politics, gender,
religion and national security. The cast of characters in
these chapters cuts across class, caste and community –
from the Brahmin students of Madras seeking admissions
to college to the local politician in Gorakhpur who
unabashedly criticized his MLA, and from the powerful
Adivasi woman who was the victim of a heinous crime
to the Delhi professor who took a state government to
court for establishing an armed civilian movement.

The question of case selection is a bugbear for any
volume that analyses a discrete group of cases or examples.

I do not make any claims of scientific precision. If you were to ask five lawyers for their list of ten forgotten cases, you would probably have five very different-looking lists, with some overlap. Put simply, while the cases considered in this book involved important legal issues, their significance transcended the legal questions that arose for the courts' consideration. This may be because of the political consequences of a case, the social impact that the case had (or didn't have), or the way in which the case was depicted in the press. Time plays an interesting role in separating landmark cases from forgotten ones. The lapse of time results in some cases fading into oblivion, and reinforces and strengthens the significance of others. In other words, 'forgotten' does not necessarily mean 'old'. While two cases considered in this book are from the early 1950s, five others are from the 1990s.

To those readers that are lawyers or legal scholars trained in India, I have written this book in the hope that it also has something to offer you. Many of you will know something about each of the cases considered in this book. Indeed, some of you may know quite a bit about the legal questions at issue in the ten 'forgotten' cases. This book is not intended to be merely a 'plain language' translation of selected Supreme Court and high court cases. Rather, it aims to bring the narratives of each of those cases to life through news reports and other contemporaneous sources. You probably know in whose favour the court made its decision, but you may not know that a police band had ironically been commissioned to play the tunes of victory to celebrate the expected *failure* of the state prosecution (see the chapter on the R.D. Bajaj case). The chapters in this book either seek to tell a story that is untold, or narrate a known story from a different perspective.

This book deviates from the dominant narrative about the role of courts in two important ways. First, it avoids the well-trodden path of nostalgia and optimism about the role of the Supreme Court and high courts in protecting fundamental rights and preserving Indian democracy. There is a large body of work that extols the role of our constitutional courts in safeguarding us from the indiscretions and misadventures of Parliament and the government. This narrative is only partially true, and is often misleading. On several occasions, the courts have remained silent and failed to prevent these misadventures. On still other occasions, the courts have created, catalysed or contributed to these misadventures. This book includes many examples of circumstances in which courts have abdicated or misused their responsibility in this way.

Second, this book seeks to dispel the myth that courts have the 'final word' on all the questions that arise for their determination. Conventional wisdom dictates that while legislatures and governments enact legislation and make policy decisions, courts finally and decisively adjudicate on their constitutionality and legality. This paints a simplistic picture of what is, in practice, far more complicated and messy. Courts' decisions are better conceived as forming part of a broader socio-political landscape. Courts depend on the cooperation of other branches of government, as well as society at large, to ensure the entrenchment of (and compliance with) their judgements. As you will see, some of the judgements considered in this book have been deeply entrenched and have exerted their influence for decades. Others have simply never been implemented, or barely survived for weeks before being swiftly consigned to the archives.

Part 1

Politics

1

The Keshav Singh Case

Who would have thought that a pamphlet distributed by a local politician would paralyse administrative machinery, strain relations between state institutions and provoke a constitutional crisis? This is precisely what happened in 1964. It took the collective efforts of several Supreme Court judges, high court judges, MPs and MLAs, and, ultimately, the prime minister and chief justice of India to restore equilibrium. This chapter presents the events leading up to and following the crisis that arose towards the end of Nehru's tenure as prime minister.

~

Keshav Singh was a resident of Gorakhpur in Uttar Pradesh, about 300 kilometres east of the state capital,

Lucknow. He was a worker of the Socialist Party, an opposition party of 'much noise but little electoral success'[1] in Uttar Pradesh. On one occasion, he successfully generated some 'noise' among opposition ranks and in the Congress party, which governed the state, by publishing a pamphlet in collaboration with two of his colleagues. This pamphlet, entitled 'Exposing the Misdeeds of Narsingh Narain Pandey',[2] alleged that Pandey, a Congress party MLA, was corrupt. The pamphlet was signed by its three authors, and distributed locally in Gorakhpur as well as in the vicinity of the legislative assembly in Lucknow.

This pamphlet did not go down well with the Congress party MLAs or Pandey, who once listed the reading of books (but not pamphlets) as one of his recreational activities.[3] They complained that the pamphlet constituted a breach of privilege, that is, the rights and immunities enjoyed by the assembly and its members. Keshav Singh and his colleagues were ordered to appear before the assembly in Lucknow to receive a reprimand. For Keshav Singh, complying with this order would have required making a railway journey of several hours from Gorakhpur to Lucknow. While his colleagues appeared before the assembly and accepted a reprimand on 19 February 1964, Keshav Singh failed to do so, citing a lack of funds to make the journey. The assembly then decided that what could not be procured voluntarily must be acquired by force. Singh was arrested and brought to the assembly on 14 March.

The matter would have ended there had Singh done the same as his co-pamphleteers and silently allowed himself to be reprimanded. But he had other ideas. When the speaker of the assembly repeatedly asked Singh to confirm his name, he refused to answer. He stood with his back turned to the speaker, and remained silent as questions were posed to him. Matters got even worse after this. The speaker brought to the attention of the assembly a letter that would cause further consternation among Congress MLAs. Singh had written a letter to the speaker protesting against the reprimand, confirming that the statements in the pamphlet were accurate, and condemning the warrant for his arrest as 'Nadirshahi' (tyrannical). By then, the MLAs had heard enough, and Chief Minister Sucheta Kripalani moved a motion in the assembly for Singh to be imprisoned for seven days. While some members of the assembly were eager for a stricter punishment (of three months) to set a precedent, others were conscious that imprisonment may be perceived as unduly harsh, and that Singh should be discharged on condition of an apology. The assembly eventually passed a resolution in the form proposed by the chief minister, and Singh was taken to prison for his week-long sentence.

Until 18 March, the dispute between Singh and Congress MLAs was confined to a local political squabble, at best offering fodder for gossip within political circles in Uttar Pradesh. However, matters were escalated significantly the following day. Just one day before he was due to be released upon the completion of his sentence, an advocate filed a petition on behalf of Singh at the Allahabad High Court, seeking his immediate release. The petition was premised on the argument that Singh's imprisonment was illegal as he was offered no opportunity to defend himself after he was reprimanded, and that the assembly lacked the authority to commit him to prison.

Singh's petition first arose for hearing at the high court at 2 p.m., before a bench of two judges – Justices Nasirullah Beg and G.D. Sehgal. Singh's advocate – B. Solomon – appeared on his behalf, while K.N. Kapur, an assistant government advocate, represented the state government. It was agreed that the hearing should proceed an hour later on the same day. However, when the case arose for hearing at 3 p.m., Kapur did not show up and the government remained unrepresented. Kapur was thought to be briefing the secretary to the judicial department of the Uttar Pradesh government about developments in the court at the time. It was not clear whether his failure to return to the court in time was by accident or design. Based on the facts and arguments presented by Solomon, the high court ordered that his client be released on bail, subject to conditions – including that Singh attend court at every future hearing.

The first reaction of the bureaucracy in Uttar Pradesh was to treat this as they would any other case. It was suggested that the government appear at the next hearing of the case and file affidavits in the usual way. However, the speaker of the assembly's reaction to the order was not quite as sanguine. The speaker, himself a lawyer, perceived the court's approach as contrary to the separation of powers. One of the ways in which the separation of powers among the legislature, executive and judiciary was meant to be sustained was by allowing each branch autonomy in the exercise of its core functions, without interference from the others. In the speaker's view, the high court's order undermined the assembly's exclusive authority to address a breach of its own privileges.

The speaker went a step further, indicating that those directly associated with the order – including Singh, Solomon, and Justices Beg and Sehgal – had breached the privileges of the assembly. It was just as well that others, such as the administrative officers in the high court that facilitated the filing of the case, were spared. Just two days after the court's order, the assembly passed a resolution by an overwhelming majority that Singh remain in prison and be brought back to the assembly to answer for the petition filed in the high court. Astoundingly, the resolution also ordered that Solomon and the two high court judges be brought in custody before the assembly to answer for their own indiscretions.

At this stage, the skirmish between Singh and the assembly transformed into a serious battle among constitutional institutions. Singh's role as the original instigator was now forgotten, as the political community shifted its focus on how this unprecedented confrontation would play out. How would the judges respond? Would Justices Beg and Sehgal make the journey from Allahabad to Lucknow? A number of strategic and prudential considerations were now in play. If the judges agreed to appear before the assembly, the episode would risk undermining the independence of the judiciary. On the other hand, if they appeared and offered a robust defence, the assembly might be left with no choice but to refrain from further action, lest it be criticized for persecuting well-intentioned judges. Another option was for the judges themselves to file a petition in the high court, but there was no gainsaying that the judges who heard *that* petition would meet the same fate.

Justices Beg and Sehgal were not notified of this resolution through official channels. Instead, they learnt of it through a broadcast on All India Radio that evening. Any apprehensions of a mistaken report were cast aside the next morning, when the resolution was reported in the *Northern India Patrika*. The judges were conscious of the importance of taking prompt action. They filed petitions in the Allahabad High Court claiming that the resolution passed by the assembly violated Article 211 of the Constitution, which prohibited discussions of the conduct of any judge of a high court or the Supreme Court in state assemblies. Justices Beg and Sehgal requested that the implementation of the resolution against them be suspended while the case remained pending before the court. Advocate and legal scholar Jagdish Swarup, who was later appointed solicitor general of India, represented the judges.[4]

These proceedings presented difficulties for the Allahabad High Court. The chief justice of the high court (and in his absence, the most senior judge after the chief justice) is entrusted with the responsibility of case allocation. Since Chief Justice M.C. Desai was away, it fell upon the next most senior judge to allocate the case to a bench. He was reluctant to do so fearing that the bench would suffer similar consequences at the hands of the assembly. Ultimately, Jagdish Swarup offered an ingenious solution to the chief justice: that *all* the judges of the high court (aside from Justices Beg and Sehgal) should sit together to hear this case. This was not just a symbolic gesture of solidarity. The chief justice saw practical merit in the suggestion: 'the legislature will have to decide to arrest all the judges if they really persist in that course of action.'[5] The high court had just raised the stakes. Securing the custody of two judges was one thing, attempting to do so for every judge of the high court was quite another.

Chief Justice Desai returned to Allahabad, and a bench of twenty-eight judges was allocated to hear this case. This was the largest number of judges allocated to decide a case in a high court or the Supreme Court at the time. This record still stands over five decades later. The most significant decision in the Indian Supreme Court's history – the Kesavananda Bharati case[6] – was allocated to a bench of less than half the number of judges deciding this case. Courtrooms were not designed to accommodate benches of this size, making the seating arrangements for judges rather complex. Even though the chief justice's courtroom in Allahabad was large, chairs had to be arranged to seat the judges in two rows, rather than one (as is usually the case).[7] Unsurprisingly, the high court admitted the petitions filed by the judges, and restrained the government from securing the execution of arrest warrants against them. Solomon filed a petition shortly thereafter, with similar success. Keshav Singh did not get similar protection.

It was then the assembly's turn to respond, and it did

so by partially retreating from its original position. The assembly passed a resolution indicating that it required the presence of Keshav Singh, Solomon and the two judges to explain their position to the house. However, the warrants for the arrest of Solomon and Justices Beg and Sehgal were withdrawn on the grounds that the assembly's intention at that stage was to ascertain the facts from them.

These decisions and counter-decisions led to much confusion and uncertainty among the police and the administrative machinery of the state. The precise nature of the relationship between the assembly and the court was unclear to most public officials. If the police escorted the two judges and Solomon to the assembly, they would be complying with the resolution of the assembly but possibly in contempt of court. If they refused to do so, the police would be complying with the court's order but defying the resolution of the assembly. The divisional commissioner of Lucknow proceeded on leave to buy time in the midst of uncertainty. He is understood to have sought legal advice on the appropriate course of action.

By this time, the episode in Uttar Pradesh was being discussed in the corridors of power in Delhi. The chief minister apprised Prime Minister Nehru of the situation. It was decided that a 'presidential reference' would be made to the Supreme Court, to enable the court to rule decisively on the authority of the assembly on the one hand, and the courts on the other, to determine the scope of the privileges of the assembly. A presidential reference made under Article 143 of the Constitution enables the President (on the instructions of the central government) to seek the opinion of the Supreme Court on questions of law or fact. This was the fifth presidential reference to the Supreme Court since the Constitution was enacted. It was interesting that the government decided that the Supreme Court (rather than the assembly or Parliament) should clarify and decide this issue.

A number of questions were referred to the Supreme Court for its consideration. These included whether Justices Beg and Sehgal had the authority to consider Keshav Singh's petition, whether Solomon and the judges were in contempt of the assembly, and whether the assembly could lawfully direct the judges and Solomon to appear before it. A bench of seven judges, led by Chief Justice Gajendragadkar, was constituted to hear the case. The composition of the bench attracted some controversy. The chief justice had made a public statement – in the context of the Keshav Singh case – that no single institution should have custodianship of the Constitution, and that the Constitution itself was the supreme law of the land.[8] This started conversations within government about whether the chief justice leaned in favour of the high court judges and a discussion on objecting to his presence on the bench hearing the case. That course was ultimately avoided, as it was recognized that it would not be wise to develop a further confrontation within the existing confrontation.

Since this case involved matters of principle that extended beyond the state of Uttar Pradesh, the Supreme Court issued notices of hearing to all high courts and state assemblies. As expected, several prominent advocates were on display at the Supreme Court. The greatest constitutional scholar of the time, H.M. Seervai, represented the Uttar Pradesh Assembly. He was assisted by Tehmtan Andhyarujina, who would later become solicitor general of India. Andhyarujina later said that over two months were spent preparing the case, which included a thorough review of cases from England, Australia and the United States.[9] The high court judges were represented by M.C. Setalvad, himself a distinguished advocate and former attorney general of India. (Setalvad's representation turned out to be pro bono by accident, prompted by a dispute over his fee with the state government, which was meant to foot the judges' legal expenses.[10])

Finally, the stage was set for one of the most fascinating cases during Nehru's tenure. The Supreme Court was conscious that although the dispute involved a high court and legislative assembly, the implications of the decision would extend to Parliament and the Supreme Court itself. In Chief Justice Gajendragadkar's words, the objectivity of the court's approach was 'on trial'.[11] He announced the court's intention to uphold its obligation to faithfully interpret the Constitution, regardless of outcome:

> If ultimately we come to the conclusion that the view pressed before us by Mr. Setalvad for [the] High Court is erroneous, we would not hesitate to pronounce our verdict against that view. On the other hand, if we ultimately come to the conclusion that the claim made by Mr. Seervai for the House cannot be sustained, we would not falter to pronounce our verdict accordingly. In dealing with problems of this importance and significance, it is essential that we should proceed to discharge our duty without fear or favour, affection or ill-will.[12]

That outcome would be shaped by how the court interpreted two significant provisions of the Constitution. The first was Article 194(3), which stated that the powers, privileges and immunities of state legislatures should be defined by law. However, until they were defined by law, they would be the same as those of the House of Commons of the United Kingdom. This was one of many provisions of the Constitution that set out a default position, but allowed that position to be dislodged by ordinary law (rather than a formal amendment to the Constitution). Since no law codifying the privileges of Parliament or the state legislatures had been enacted at the time, the privileges, powers and immunities of the House of Commons would apply.

The interpretation of British cases on parliamentary privilege therefore formed a focal point of the dispute between the assembly and the high court. These cases included one from 1704 in which the House of Commons had deprived four men of the right to vote and committed them to prison;[13] another from 1750 when a prisoner refused to kneel at the bar of the house;[14] and an 1839 case involving a defamation claim against 'Hansard', the publisher of parliamentary debates.[15] The leading textbook on parliamentary privilege in Britain, written by Erskine May, former clerk of the House of Commons (analogous to the chief executive), was cited as an authoritative text by the Supreme Court.[16]

However, the Supreme Court was confronted by an additional complication in India. It was argued on behalf of Singh that parliamentary privileges were being exercised in disregard of his right to personal liberty under Article 21 of the Constitution. It was suggested that in the event of a conflict between the right to personal liberty and parliamentary privileges, the former should prevail. The Supreme Court agreed, noting that while these two constitutional provisions should be construed harmoniously to the extent possible, Article 21 would prevail in the event of an inconsistency.

The second constitutional provision at issue was Article 211. This provision imposed an absolute prohibition on discussion of the conduct of judges of the Supreme Court or high courts in state legislatures. It was argued on behalf of the high court judges that the assembly resolution requiring their appearance to provide an explanation for their conduct violated this provision. The Supreme Court agreed, noting that the assembly's resolution was an affront to the independence of the judiciary. Article 211 could not be reduced to a 'meaningless declaration', for it was part of the essential apparatus that ensured that the courts could take difficult, even if incorrect, decisions without fear of political retribution.

Overall, the conclusions in the majority opinion of Chief Justice Gajendragadkar were decisively in favour of the high court. The Supreme Court held that it was within the authority of the high court to consider Keshav Singh's petition, and to release him on bail until it arrived at a decision. Just as Keshav Singh and his advocate Solomon did not commit contempt of the house by bringing proceedings, the high court judges did not do so by entertaining those proceedings. It was not within the authority of the assembly to issue a warrant for the arrest of, or for that matter even call for an explanation from, Solomon and Justices Beg and Sehgal. It followed that the bench of twenty-eight judges of the high court was justified in restraining the assembly from seeking the production of Solomon and the high court judges.

One of the judges wrote a dissenting opinion taking a more nuanced view of the situation. Justice Sarkar disagreed with the majority's opinion that parliamentary privileges would be subordinate to the right to personal liberty in the event of a conflict. This would not be harmonious construction, but preferring one constitutional provision to the exclusion of the other. Perhaps his most controversial conclusion was that it was within the power of the assembly to require an explanation from Solomon and Justices Beg and Sehgal. In his view, implicit in the assembly's power to punish for contempt was the power to investigate the facts to determine whether contempt had been committed in the first place. The thought of high court judges being summoned to offer explanations to the assembly did not seem to cause concern to Justice Sarkar as it did for the others.

Since Justice Sarkar held that the high court judges could have been asked to provide explanations to the assembly to ascertain if contempt had been committed, what if the judges were actually found in contempt by the assembly? Would they be entitled to immunity (under Article 211 or other constitutional provisions), or could they in fact be punished in some way? For Justice Sarkar to hold that the judges could also have been proceeded against for contempt would have been to push the envelope too far. Instead, he 'decided not to decide' this question in the hope that it would never arise: 'theoretical disputes should be allowed to lie buried in learned tracts and not be permitted to soil our daily lives.'[17]

Although their victory was not unanimous, it was clear that the high court judges and Solomon had trumped the assembly on all of the questions that were referred to the Supreme Court. Criticism of the Supreme Court's judgement streamed in soon after it was pronounced. Although this criticism took different forms, it largely boiled down to one question: did the judgement appropriately balance power between two co-equal constitutional institutions? First, the Supreme Court analysed the questions before it through a framework that left little room for a nuanced view.[18] It was possible, for example, for the Supreme Court to decide that it was beyond the authority of the high court to consider Keshav Singh's petition, but also that it was beyond the authority of the assembly to commit the judges for contempt for deciding that question. By framing this as a contest for custodianship of the Constitution, the Supreme Court left itself with little choice but to hold that the high court had the authority to decide the petition, if it wished to avoid the unsavoury outcome of high court judges being interrogated in the assembly.

The second reason for which the judgement was criticized was that the court refused to acknowledge any role for the assembly in interpreting the scope of its own privileges. This was prompted, to some extent, by the reference to the Supreme Court itself (rather than leaving the question to be decided by the assembly). However, it may not have been out of place for the court to say that it was for the assembly to interpret Article 194(3), which stated that the powers, privileges and immunities of state legislatures should be defined by law and that this was a matter of the internal functioning of the assembly. The assembly was itself a democratically elected institution that was accountable to the electorate of the state. Instead, the court took it upon itself to interpret that provision, signalling that it would be the authoritative interpreter of all parts of the Constitution – even those that addressed one branch exclusively.

The most significant criticism of the Supreme Court's decision focused on the interplay between fundamental rights and parliamentary privileges. In a previous case only a few years before the Supreme Court's decision, the court had arrived at a different view.[19] A Patna daily called *Searchlight* had published a portion of the proceedings of the Bihar Assembly that had been expunged. A notice for breach of privilege was issued, and the editor of *Searchlight* argued that parliamentary privileges would yield to the fundamental right to freedom of speech and expression in the event of a conflict. At that time the court disagreed with this position.

In the Keshav Singh reference, the Supreme Court took the opposite view – that parliamentary privilege would yield to the fundamental right to personal liberty. However, it did so without overturning the decision in the *Searchlight* case. As a consequence, the legal position was that parliamentary privilege would trump some fundamental rights, but not others. These decisions skewed the incentives of legislatures to codify the law on privileges. Parliament and the state assemblies now lacked an incentive to codify privileges into law, as this law, being ordinary, would be inferior to all (rather than just some) fundamental rights. The result therefore was that even though the Constitution contemplated the codification of parliamentary privileges, this codification has never taken place.

Paradoxically, over seventy years after Indian independence, privileges continue to remain tied to those of the House of Commons as they were in January 1950. Although a cosmetic amendment was made to Article 194 to eliminate the reference to the House of Commons in 1978, its effect remains much the same.[20] Dr Rajendra Prasad's statement in the Constituent Assembly that 'Parliament may never legislate' on this issue and that the members should 'be vigilant' was prescient.[21] That was not by accident, but for good reason. The political calculation has always been that the legislatures have little to gain, but much to lose, by codification. Had the judgement in the *Searchlight* case been decisively overturned, privileges may well have been codified as the Constitution contemplated.

The Supreme Court's decision was not received well by Parliament and state legislative assemblies across the country. The decision was heavily criticized at a Conference of Presiding Officers of Legislative Bodies held in Bombay in January 1965. The conference resolved that the Supreme Court 'reduced legislatures to the status of inferior courts' and negated the intentions of the framers of the Constitution. It was therefore recommended that the Constitution be amended to make clear that legislatures have the exclusive authority to adjudicate and punish cases of contempt, whether committed by a member or a stranger, and whether inside or outside the assembly.

Counter-efforts were made by lawyers and bar associations to educate the public about the judgement and clarify any misconceptions. This included a statement signed by a group of lawyers and public intellectuals, including Setalvad, followed by a published brochure. The Bar Association of India also organized a symposium chaired by Pandit H.N. Kunzru, a distinguished parliamentarian and leader of the freedom movement. Setalvad's speech at the symposium played down the narrative of conflict between the legislature and the judiciary, with Setalvad describing the case as a recalibration between citizens' rights and the rights of the legislatures.[22] Ultimately, the proposals to amend the Constitution were not pursued, and the Supreme Court's judgement remained intact.

There was still the small matter of Keshav Singh's petition being decided by the high court. The judgement turned out to be anticlimactic, for the high court held that there was no reason to believe that the assembly's decision was in bad faith and that it lacked the jurisdiction to entertain Singh's petition.[23] Upon concluding that the assembly had the power to imprison for contempt and impose the sentence it did on Singh, the court would not consider the propriety or legality of the assembly's decision. Keshav Singh was sent back to prison to serve out the last day of his sentence.

What was remarkable about this case is that the disagreements between the high court and the Uttar Pradesh Assembly would never have intensified in the way that they did had it not been for a series of mistakes and errors of judgement. It was curious enough that Singh's lawyer filed a petition with only one day left on his sentence. Had the government's advocate returned to the high court at 3 p.m. (as he had promised), he would have likely explained the circumstances to the court, and Singh's bail may have been denied at the outset. Instead, the high court benefited from only Singh's side of the story. Had the assembly responded by entering an appearance in court and apprising it of the full set of facts – rather than responding by passing a resolution in respect of Singh, Solomon and Justices Beg and Sehgal – the matter may have concluded there. Instead, institutions continued to respond defensively as the situation moved further along the ladder of escalation. This case is worth remembering – if for nothing else, to demonstrate how easily constitutional institutions can turn against one another and, equally, how difficult problems are best solved through statesmanship rather than brinksmanship.

2

Minerva Mills
v
Union of India

On 24 April 1973, the Supreme Court made its most significant decision in history. Prime Minister Indira Gandhi enjoyed a majority in Parliament that was large enough for her to have constitutional amendments enacted with ease. An 'iterative game of action–response–rejoinder'[1] was playing out between the Congress government and the Supreme Court. No sooner did the court pass a judgement that was unpalatable to the establishment than the government began exploring methods to nullify it, including through amendments to the Constitution. This battle for custodianship of the Constitution reached a crescendo when a Supreme Court panel of an unprecedented size – thirteen judges – was tasked in the Kesavananda Bharati case with deciding whether there were any limits on Parliament's power to amend the Constitution. The court held, by a narrow majority of seven to six, that Parliament lacked the power to amend the basic structure or essential features of the Constitution.

The Kesavananda case, however, is not the subject of this chapter. This book would not be honest to its title if it were, as this case is etched deeply in the public consciousness. The civics syllabus for some school examinations does not include any case law, with this being the only exception. The Minerva Mills case followed soon after and was arguably as significant as the Kesavananda case. It is well known among lawyers, but much less so among the general public.

Indira Gandhi was not pleased with the Supreme Court's attempt in the Kesavananda case to insulate the Constitution from root-and-branch transformation. Over the next few years, her response was threefold: first, to punish the judges who curtailed government power; second, to attempt judicial reversal of the judgement in the Kesavananda case; and third, to attempt legislative reversal. The punishment was forfeiture of the office of chief justice, as Justices Shelat, Hegde and Grover (all of whom held against the government in the Kesavananda case) were overlooked for the position. The judicial reversal was attempted during the Emergency, when another panel of thirteen judges was assembled to reconsider the decision. The reconsideration was 'suddenly and inexplicably abandoned' on the third day into the hearing.[2]

The attempted legislative reversal also took place during the Emergency. The 42nd Amendment to the Constitution, enacted in 1976, was less an amendment and more an effort to radically transform the nature of the Constitution. It added two clauses to Article 368 of the Constitution (the provision governing constitutional amendments) with a view to overturning the Kesavananda judgement and making clear 'beyond doubt'[3] that Parliament had the power to amend *any* part of the Constitution. The first clause stated that no amendment of the Constitution, regardless of when it was enacted, would be 'called in question in any court on any ground'.[4] The second clause clarified that there would be 'no limitation whatever'[5] on Parliament's power to amend the Constitution.

Once Indira Gandhi called (and famously lost) the elections of 1977, the Janata government engaged in an effort to undo the damage to the Constitution. It succeeded in some respects but failed in others. The changes proposed included amendments to Article 368 that would identify the following as forming part of the basic structure of the Constitution: independence of the judiciary, free and fair elections, and all fundamental rights within the Constitution. Under the proposed amendment, changes to this basic structure could only be undertaken upon approval in a referendum.[6] However, the government failed to galvanize the two-thirds majority required in the Congress-dominated Rajya Sabha, and the amendment was dropped. The battle over which aspects of the Constitution could be amended (and how) was left for another day.

~

Established in the early twentieth century, Minerva Mills was a textile mill located near the Bangalore city railway station. Its many workers included the father of Nandan Nilekani, who would one day become the CEO of Infosys Technologies.[7] The Congress government had nationalized it in the early 1970s claiming that it was mismanaged.[8] In 1977, the erstwhile owners approached the Supreme Court to challenge its nationalization.

At around the time the case was filed, Nani Palkhivala, India's foremost constitutional litigator who also appeared against the Congress government in the Kesavananda case, was appointed ambassador to the United States by the Janata government. Soon after his appointment was announced, Palkhivala said in a telephone interview to the *New York Times*: 'My thinking does indeed seem to be in line with the thinking of President Carter, and the American people, on things like human rights.'[9] However, Palkhivala soon felt the urge to return to India to protect human rights through the courts, and resumed practice in time to argue the Minerva Mills case on behalf of the previous owners.

At its heart, the case involved the government's nationalization powers and the right to property. However, the fundamental right to property under the Constitution had just been deleted in accordance with the Janata Party's election manifesto.[10] The precise reasons for which the right was deleted are unclear, although it was speculated that the manifesto pledge was made to secure the political support of the communist parties and others.[11] Palkhivala devised the strategy of arguing the case by challenging the Congress government's amendments to the Constitution rather than the Janata amendments. Instead of arguing that the (Janata government's) constitutional amendment deleting the right to property was itself unconstitutional because it violated the basic structure of the Constitution, he used the case as a vehicle to challenge constitutional amendments passed during Indira Gandhi's tenure as prime minister.

The Congress government had secured amendments to Article 368 of the Constitution to give Parliament unfettered powers to amend the Constitution and also to take away the jurisdiction of the courts to review such amendments. Therefore, the first issue for the court's consideration in the Minerva Mills case was whether the amendments to the Constitution adding two new clauses to Article 368 (with a view to nullifying the Kesavananda judgement) were valid. (If these amendments were invalid, then the Janata government's amendments deleting the right to property as a fundamental right would also be open to judicial scrutiny.) Palkhivala aimed to do in the Supreme Court what the Janata government failed to do politically – nullify the Congress government's constitutional amendment overruling the Kesavananda judgement. The specific circumstances of the Bangalore mill soon fell into the background, with the vexed question of whether there were any limits at all on Parliament's power to amend the Constitution once again taking centre stage.

The amendments to Article 368 presented a formidable obstacle to the Kesavananda judgement. The reason for this was that although seven of the thirteen judges in the Kesavananda case held that Parliament lacked the power to alter the basic structure of the Constitution, they arrived at this conclusion for different reasons.

While some of the judgements were based on the idea that the word 'amendment' could not mean replacement with a practically new and different Constitution, others noted that the limitation on Parliament's power to amend the Constitution was implied in the scheme of the Constitution.[12] By specifically clarifying that the power to 'amend' was boundless, the Congress government's amendments appeared to decisively address the first set of judgements.

Palkhivala formulated three powerful arguments in seeking to convince the Supreme Court to dislodge the amendments. First, 'the donee of a limited power cannot, by the exercise of that very power, convert the limited power into an unlimited one'.[13] To do so would allow Parliament, a creature of the Constitution, to become its master. Second, the limited amending power was itself a basic feature of the Constitution. Following the court's decision in the Kesavananda case, Parliament had no authority to disturb that feature. Third, by stating that no court would have the power to pronounce upon the validity of a constitutional amendment, the amendment damaged the balance of power between the judiciary and Parliament.

Palkhivala used the Minerva Mills case as a platform to challenge another Emergency-era amendment to the Constitution. The Congress government had secured an amendment to Article 31C of the Constitution which protected from the scrutiny of two fundamental rights (the rights to equality and freedom) all laws that gave effect to any of the directive principles under the Constitution. In other words, no law that gave effect to one or more of the directive principles could be struck down by a court on the basis that it violated, say, the right to freedom of speech or the right to equality.

Palkhivala's argument against this amendment was based on principle and pragmatism. Article 31C embodied the 'quintessence of authoritarianism': the difference between authoritarianism and democracy was that 'the former subordinates human freedoms to directive principles of state policy, while the latter achieves the same objectives while respecting human freedoms'.[14] In practical terms, to limit Article 31C to laws that gave effect to directive principles was meaningless, as the directive principles covered the whole spectrum of governance. Almost every law enacted by the government could be associated, in one way or another, with a directive principle.

By the time the Minerva Mills case arose for hearing, Morarji Desai's Janata Party government had fallen and a 'caretaker' government (led by Prime Minister Charan Singh) was in place until the conclusion of the next general elections. Attorney General L.N. Sinha and Additional

Solicitor General K.K. Venugopal argued the case on behalf of the government. In Sinha and Venugopal, Palkhivala faced formidable opposing counsel. Sinha was a stalwart of the bar who was 'hero-worshipped'[15] by young lawyers at the time. Venugopal was a rising star who would go on to practise at the Supreme Court for over five decades and be appointed attorney general by the Modi government in 2017.

As law officers during the Charan Singh government, Sinha and Venugopal were in the precarious position of defending constitutional amendments that were made by the Congress government during the Emergency. Their initial response to Palkhivala's arguments was to seek to persuade the court that the questions Palkhivala raised did not arise from the facts of the Minerva Mills case at all.[16] They also argued that Article 31C reinforced rather than undermined the basic structure of the Constitution. This was because the directive principles provided goals in the absence of which fundamental rights 'would be meaningless'.[17] Responding to Palkhivala's argument that Article 31C's protective blanket would be all-encompassing, Venugopal submitted charts to the Supreme Court illustrating decided cases involving laws that would not have been saved by Article 31C.[18] It has long been suspected – but never definitively established – that Sinha and Venugopal were instructed by the government to defend the nationalization of Minerva Mills in general terms, while at the same time doing little to protect the Congress government's amendments to the Constitution.[19]

The hearing took place before a bench of five judges of the Supreme Court, headed by Chief Justice Y.V. Chandrachud. Justice Chandrachud formed part of the group of judges that rejected the basic structure doctrine in the Kesavananda case. Also on the bench were Justices A.C. Gupta, N.L. Untwalia, P.N. Bhagwati and P.S. Kailasam. The hearing lasted twenty days, from 22 October 1979 to 16 November 1979.[20] Although this seemed long enough, it was dwarfed by the length of the Kesavananda case hearing (which had taken place over sixty-eight days in 1972–73).[21] After the hearing concluded but before the judgement was pronounced, the Congress party returned to power with a comfortable majority, with Indira Gandhi sworn in as prime minister yet again.

About six months passed without the judgement having been delivered. Perhaps conscious that the significant delay would only be exacerbated by the upcoming summer vacation, the court decided to issue its decision with 'fuller reasons to follow' after the vacation.[22] Writing on behalf of four judges, Chief Justice Chandrachud noted that both amendments (the amendments to Articles 368 and 31C) were beyond the amending power of Parliament and violated the basic structure of the Constitution. At this stage, a fault line emerged among the judges on the panel. Rather than signing on the decision of four of the judges on the last day before the vacation, Justice Bhagwati preferred to defer his own decision until the reopening of the court after summer. For Bhagwati, questions of 'grave and momentous consequence' were better left to a fully 'reasoned judgment'.[23] Implicit in this was a criticism of the other judges for issuing an 'unreasoned' judgement in haste before the court closed for summer.

As would have been expected, upon the reopening of the court after the summer vacation, two judgements were delivered. Chief Justice Chandrachud delivered the majority judgement on behalf of all the judges except Justice Bhagwati, who wrote a separate opinion. Justice Chandrachud struck down both amendments to the Constitution, in line with the decision issued on the eve of the summer vacation.

On the amendment to Parliament's power to amend the Constitution (Article 368), Justice Chandrachud noted that the amendment gave Parliament a 'vast and undefined' power to amend the Constitution, even to the extent of distorting it out of recognition. In theory, this unlimited power to amend the Constitution could be relied upon to eliminate democracy and establish a totalitarian state. Had the amendment been upheld, there would have been no legal (or judicially imposed) limits on Parliament's power to subvert democracy through a constitutional amendment. The only limits on the power to amend the Constitution would have been political – which did not inspire confidence in an era of single-party dominance. Palkhivala's argument that Parliament could not enlarge a limited amending power into an unlimited one also won the day.

Following the Kesavananda case, 'ouster clauses' (which attempted to insulate categories of law enacted by Parliament from judicial scrutiny) were the most likely candidates to be struck down for damaging the basic structure of the Constitution. In fact, in the Kesavananda case itself, an ouster clause in Article 31C of the Constitution (as it then was), which restricted the court from even *considering* whether a law was enacted to give effect to certain directive principles when the legislature simply *asserted* that it had this effect, was struck down. And so it was with the amendment to Article 368 which attempted to eliminate any inquiry into the validity of constitutional amendments. For Justice Chandrachud, this amendment deprived citizens of 'one of the most valuable modes of redress' under the Constitution – the right to petition the Supreme Court in respect of a violation of fundamental rights.

Justice Chandrachud struck down the amendments to Article 31C of the Constitution in equally emphatic terms. The primary reason for this aspect of the court's judgement was that it disturbed the balance between fundamental rights and directive principles. Just as the fundamental rights would be without a 'radar and a compass' without the directive principles, the directive principles would be a 'pretence for tyranny' if they came at the cost of fundamental rights. On a practical level, the court apprehended that Parliament could use Article 31C as a conduit to protect a large number of laws from full judicial scrutiny.

The opinion concluded with the following passage:

Three Articles of our Constitution, and only three, stand between the heaven of freedom into which Tagore wanted his country to awake and the abyss of unrestrained power. They are Articles 14, 19 and 21. Article 31C has removed two sides of that golden triangle which affords to the people of this country an assurance that the promise held forth by the Preamble will be performed by ushering an egalitarian era through the discipline of fundamental rights, that is, without emasculation of the rights to liberty and equality.[24]

This majority opinion especially provoked debate since Justice Chandrachud had, in an opinion from seven years earlier in the Kesavananda case, rejected the very same basic structure doctrine which he now cited favourably to strike down constitutional amendments. While some criticized Justice Chandrachud for his 'rhetoric on sanctity of fundamental rights [in the Minerva Mills judgement]' soon after his opinion in the Kesavananda judgement,[25] others described his journey as a 'pilgrim's progress' to the shrine of the basic structure of the Constitution.[26]

On the one hand, it might well be said that Justice Chandrachud was compelled by judicial discipline to uphold the basic structure doctrine in the Minerva Mills judgement, seeing as the doctrine was established by a much larger panel of the Supreme Court in the Kesavananda judgement. While this may have been true from a moral and political perspective, it was not quite as clear from a legal perspective. First, scholars had debated long and hard whether the basic structure doctrine was actually endorsed by a majority of judges in the Kesavananda judgement. Many took the view that there was no 'majority' view at all – of the thirteen judges, six judges concluded that there were *no limitations* on Parliament's power to amend the Constitution; six others concluded that there were *implied limitations* on Parliament's power to amend the Constitution; and the final judge, Justice H.R. Khanna, held that while there were no such implied limitations, an 'amendment' to the Constitution necessarily excluded any attempts to abrogate its identity. The absence of a clear majority view might have been a way to sidestep the Kesavananda judgement, but it was not deployed. Second, it was arguable that the constitutional amendment to Article 368 had eliminated the basis for the basic structure doctrine, which relied in some measure on the text of the Constitution itself.[27] There also proved to be no appetite for this argument. Thus, Chief Justice Chandrachud upheld the basic structure doctrine (in contrast with his earlier view) despite an opportunity to overturn it.

While the outcome of the majority decision was known in advance, Justice Bhagwati's was not. Justice Bhagwati agreed with the majority's decision striking down Parliament's amendment of Article 368, but disagreed with the decision striking down the amendment to Article 31C. On the first issue, Justice Bhagwati was persuaded by Palkhivala's argument that Parliament could not transform a limited amending power into an unlimited one – to do so was a 'futile exercise'. On the second issue, he offered a strong rebuttal to the other judges, noting that the fundamental rights had no meaning to the poor and marginalized in the absence of directive principles. Echoing Sinha's and Venugopal's arguments, he noted that the amendment to Article 31C of the Constitution did not damage the basic structure of the Constitution, but strengthened and reinforced it.

As it happened, the erstwhile owners of Minerva Mills continued to contest the nationalization on different grounds, only to ultimately fail at the Supreme Court in September 1986.[28]

~

The Minerva Mills case undoubtedly set the tone for the future of the basic structure doctrine in India. However, it also brought to light the uncomfortable dynamics among the two most senior judges of the Supreme Court. Justice Bhagwati's complaints about the way in which the case was managed (foreshadowed in his decision from the last day before the vacation) were more fully expressed in his substantive judgement issued after the vacation. Citing Justice Chandrachud's own complaint in the Kesavananda case that there was no opportunity for a 'free and frank exchange of thoughts' among the judges before judgement was handed down, he noted:

I hoped that after the completion of the argument on questions of such momentous significance, there would be a 'free and frank exchange of thoughts' in a judicial conference either before or after the draft judgment was circulated by my Lord the Chief Justice and I would either be able to share the views of my colleagues or if that was not possible, at least try to persuade them to agree with my point of view. But, I find myself in the same predicament in which the learned Chief Justice found himself [in the Kesavananda case].[29]

Asked about Justice Bhagwati's criticism in an interview after his retirement, Justice Chandrachud admitted that the judges did not have the chance to review one another's draft judgements, but noted that they had several opportunities to exchange views about the case. Other judges on the panel confirmed this.[30]

This was not the only occasion in his judgement that Justice Bhagwati would accuse his colleague of double standards. He cited a passage from Justice Chandrachud's own judgement in the Kesavananda case, emphasizing that fundamental rights and directive principles of state policy both shared an equally important position in the constitutional scheme, in support of his decision to uphold Article 31C in the Minerva Mills judgement. Justice Chandrachud had noted that 'the basic object of conferring freedoms on individuals [through fundamental rights]' was to achieve the objectives set out in the directive principles.[31] Parliament was inspired, said Justice Bhagwati, by the same philosophy in making the constitutional amendment as 'the noble philosophy eloquently expressed in highly inspiring and evocative words, full of passion and feeling' by Justice Chandrachud in the Kesavananda judgement.[32] It had long been speculated that Justice Bhagwati's rancour arose from Justice Chandrachud's prior elevation to the Supreme Court (resulting in a long tenure as chief justice), even though Bhagwati had been appointed a high court judge earlier than his colleague.

Justice Bhagwati himself received a fair share of criticism both before and after the decision in the Minerva Mills case was pronounced. It transpired that after the hearing had concluded and while the case was still awaiting judgement, Justice Bhagwati wrote an effusive letter congratulating Indira Gandhi on her election victory, praising her 'iron will', 'uncanny insight and dynamic vision' and her 'heart which is identified with the misery of the poor and the weak'.[33] The criticism of failing to consult colleagues came full circle. Just as Justice Chandrachud had complained about the lack of discussion among the judges in the Kesavananda case and was at the receiving end of the same criticism in the Minerva Mills case, Justice Bhagwati made the same complaint in the Minerva Mills case and was the recipient of it in a prominent case involving judicial appointments a few years later.[34]

Even as lawyers and political commentators lamented the state of the 'bench divided',[35] the Congress government was predictably displeased with the majority decision in the Minerva Mills case. After all, the way in which the case played out was that the Congress government's amendments to the Constitution were struck down, while the Janata government's amendments remained unaffected. Law minister and MP from Secunderabad, P. Shiv Shanker, criticized the judgement at every available opportunity. On one occasion, he described the judgement as betraying a 'conservative and retrograde outlook' for the judiciary.[36] At a National Seminar on Constitutional Law held at Siddharth College, Bombay, Shiv Shanker commented – in the presence of no less than Justice Bhagwati – that had the court kept in mind the principles laid down in the Preamble, the controversy of the supremacy of fundamental rights over directive principles could have been avoided.[37]

It soon became clear that the government's reaction would not stop at displeasure. Several political parties offered suggestions and questioned the government on how it would react to the decision. One MP from the Communist Party asked whether the government would be willing to hold broad-based consultation among political parties. Shiv Shanker saw no purpose being served in such consultations. Another MP asked whether the government intended to organize a full-scale parliamentary debate on the issue – a suggestion that was also rejected. The law minister also dismissed the idea of a presidential reference seeking the advisory opinion of the Supreme Court.[38] Criticism of the judges that decided the case in the Rajya Sabha led retired Supreme Court Justice M. Hidayatullah (then vice president and, therefore, chairman of the Rajya Sabha) to remind members on several occasions of the constitutional provision[39] that prevented discussion on the conduct of judges in Parliament.[40]

Still more radical suggestions to overturn the Supreme Court's judgement were on the table. These included organizing a popular referendum on constitutional amendment,[41] and 'converting' the houses of Parliament into an interim Constituent Assembly with the power to 'amend' any provision of the Constitution, including its basic structure.[42] The option ultimately selected by the law minister was, or at least appeared, somewhat more benign. He elected to ask the Supreme Court to reconsider its decision through a review petition. According to the law minister, the timing of filing the petition was a matter of litigation 'strategy'[43] – a euphemism for filing at a moment when it was likely to arise for hearing before judges that were sympathetic to the government's position.

As it happened, the government did not wait long. About five weeks after the judgement, it filed a review petition at the Supreme Court seeking a reconsideration of the Minerva Mills judgement. Justice Bhagwati's criticism of Justice Chandrachud's management of the case turned out to be the linchpin of the government's case. The government argued that the judgement was not a decision of the court at all, but only consisted of the opinions of individual judges. This argument was innovative, but also inherently weak – for judges to consult with one another was always desirable, but never strictly necessary. Besides, it would hardly set a good precedent to allow unsuccessful litigants to have judgements reviewed based on the internal dynamics of the decision-making process.

Palkhivala described the government's attempt to have the decision reviewed as a 'shocking exhibition of the arrogance of power'.[44] He staunchly opposed the petition when it arose for hearing. His argument was that the only reason the Supreme Court was even willing to consider the petition in an oral hearing rather than dismissing it on the papers was that it had been filed by the government: '[I]f Minerva Mills had lost and filed an application of this nature, would you have entertained it?' Chief Justice

Chandrachud tried to calm Palkhivala down with some humour: 'Anyone is welcome to file an application. Someone can file a suit saying that the Supreme Court belongs to him. We will examine that too appropriately.'[45] Ultimately, the hearing was adjourned with no fixed date for the next hearing, on the basis that one of the judges on the bench, Justice Kailasam, was scheduled to retire the following day. The review petition died a natural death and the government did not ultimately pursue it.

The Minerva Mills judgement was not only unpopular within the government of the day, but it also had its share of critics on the bench. In a different case about two years later, a bench of the Supreme Court (with Justice Bhagwati being the only overlapping participant in both cases) criticized the judgement for deciding questions that did not naturally arise from the facts before it. This was, in effect, a rebuke for walking into Palkhivala's 'trap' of using the case as a vehicle to delimit Parliament's power to amend the Constitution. The court's criticism was not muffled: 'We have some misgivings about the *Minerva Mills*' decision despite its rare beauty and persuasive rhetoric.'[46] Nevertheless, no further concerted efforts were made – either through Parliament or through the courts – to overturn the Minerva Mills judgement. The judgement started off on a shaky footing, but soon became established constitutional doctrine.

The Minerva Mills judgement turned out to be as significant for the endurance of the basic structure doctrine as the Kesavananda judgement. By enabling the courts to review not just ordinary legislation but also amendments to the Constitution, the Kesavananda judgement was an extraordinary usurpation of power by the judiciary, undertaken in extraordinary circumstances. The Minerva Mills case arose in far less extraordinary circumstances – the era of Emergency and judges' supersessions had concluded and relative normalcy had been restored.

Close to four decades after the Minerva Mills judgement, the official version of the Constitution published by the government includes a small tribute to the judgement. The amendments challenged in the Minerva Mills case still formally remain part of the text, since the effect of the court's judgement is to deem them invalid and unenforceable rather than strike them out from the book altogether.[47] However, these amendments are accompanied by the following footnote: 'This section has been declared invalid by the Supreme Court.'

3

Rameshwar Prasad
v
Union of India

The next case considered in this book offers a heady combination of high political drama and significant questions of constitutional law. The Rameshwar Prasad case, and the circumstances surrounding it, involves no less than two state elections, midnight phone calls to Moscow, two Supreme Court decisions (one of them under five pages, the other close to five hundred), resignations and near-resignations, and hideaways in Jamshedpur.

~

Lalu Prasad Yadav had administered Bihar for nearly fifteen years by the time the state assembly elections came around in February 2005. He did so directly as chief minister of the state for roughly the first half of that period. For the second half, he governed the state by proxy through his wife, Rabri Devi, who assumed the position following his resignation prompted by corruption charges. Anti-incumbency was running high, and internal rebellions within Yadav's Rashtriya Janata Dal (RJD) were expected to impact its electoral fortunes.

Aside from the incumbents, at least four other political parties had credible aspirations of securing a substantial number of seats in the assembly. They were the Bharatiya Janata Party (BJP) and the Janata Dal United (JDU) – both part of the National Democratic Alliance (NDA), the Lok Janshakti Party (LJP) and the Congress. The Bihar Legislative Assembly had 243 seats, making 122 the magic number required to secure an absolute majority in the assembly and form a stable government. However, that number proved elusive. The elections yielded a hung assembly, with no party or alliance within striking distance of the magic number. The NDA secured ninety-two seats, while the RJD, the LJP and the Congress secured seventy-five, twenty-nine and ten seats respectively. Six other political parties secured at least one seat, and seventeen independent candidates were elected.

The governor of a state assumes heightened responsibility in circumstances where there is a hung assembly, as he has the authority to invite those that are most likely to cobble a majority to form the government. The role of Buta Singh, Bihar's governor, therefore became crucial following the election results. Singh was 'no novice to politics' and had aligned with different political forces over the years – including as home minister in Rajiv Gandhi's Congress government and communications minister in Atal Bihari Vajpayee's NDA government.[1] Singh held a series of meetings with political parties in the days after the election results were declared. However, he concluded that no party or alliance was in a position to mobilize a majority in the assembly. This was predominantly because the LJP, which could effectively play the role of kingmaker between the NDA on the one side and the RJD–Congress combination on the other, chose not to extend support to either.

Singh therefore wrote to the President of India recommending that President's rule be imposed in Bihar, with the assembly being kept in a state of 'suspended animation' (this meant that although the assembly would not be dissolved, it could not transact any business). The idea was that this course of action would leave more time and space for discussions and political realignments. The President accepted this recommendation, resulting in Bihar effectively being administered by the United

Progressive Alliance (UPA) government in New Delhi.

The process of political realignments envisaged by the governor was then well and truly set into motion. First, the group of seventeen independent MLAs declared their support for the NDA. Three other parties, each holding a small number of seats, followed. This took the NDA close to securing a majority in the assembly. However, in order to attain a majority, it became clear that the NDA would still require the support of some LJP or RJD or Congress MLAs. Rumours ran rife, as over a dozen MLAs from the LJP – sequestered in resorts just outside Jamshedpur[2] – were apparently being 'induced' to pledge their support to the NDA.

As these events were playing out, Singh sent two further reports to the President. The first was sent on 27 April 2005. The governor warned that the BJP and the JDU were making concerted efforts to win over MLAs from the LJP through 'various means'.[3] This 'unprincipled and opportunistic realignment' was undesirable and would distort the mandate of the electorate, the governor said. The governor concluded with the warning that in order to avoid any further horse-trading, there may be no choice but to organize a fresh round of elections in Bihar.

Singh's next report to the President was sent about four weeks later, on 21 May 2005. By that stage, the governor observed, one LJP MLA had already moved across to the JDU, with a large group of seventeen to eighteen MLAs expected to follow suit upon being offered allurements. The governor therefore recommended that the assembly be dissolved and fresh elections be called in the state.

The UPA government formally received the governor's report the next day. The rumour on the street was that the BJP and the JDU were on the brink of staking claim to the government. The UPA government had just concluded its one-year anniversary celebrations, and an emergency cabinet meeting was called at 11 p.m. that evening to consider Singh's report. The cabinet swiftly accepted the governor's recommendation and forwarded it to President A.P.J. Abdul Kalam for his assent. The President's assent was required for the dissolution of the assembly and the calling of fresh elections. As it happened, Kalam was in Moscow that evening as part of a four-nation official visit to Russia, Iceland, Switzerland and Ukraine. Kalam was woken up in the middle of the night in his room at the Kempinski Hotel with a request to sign on the dotted line.[4] The UPA presumably wanted to avoid the formation of a BJP–JDU government at all costs.

Ordinarily, a government may have waited for the President to return from his foreign trip or, at the least, left more time for the President to consider the file. Absent this luxury, Kalam had three options, each of which raised its own complications. He could return the file to the UPA government for reconsideration, although he would be obliged to sign if the file were sent back to him. Alternatively, he could have waited until he returned to Delhi – but this would have involved a delay of eight days. In that time, it was likely that the government would be formed in any event. The third option was simply to sign the file, in spite of any misgivings about whether it was appropriate to dissolve the assembly in the circumstances. In a decision that he would live to regret, Kalam chose option three.

The Bihar Assembly was dissolved within hours, and pandemonium broke loose. Ram Vilas Paswan, the president of the LJP, expelled seven of his colleagues for anti-party activities. The BJP organized dharnas and road blockades in the state following the announcement. Describing the dissolution as a 'fraud on the Constitution and murder of democracy',[5] it organized a fairly successful statewide strike in protest the next day. Senior leaders from the NDA demanded early elections in a meeting with the Election Commission.[6] Now that the assembly had been dissolved, the NDA didn't want the UPA to govern Bihar through President's rule and wanted fresh elections called at the earliest opportunity.

Together with its political strategy, the NDA's legal strategy was also set into motion. Four writ petitions were filed in the Supreme Court by candidates who had been elected to the dissolved assembly – one each by members of the BJP and the JDU, the third by a 'rebel' LJP member and the fourth by an independent candidate. They contended that the President's proclamation dissolving the assembly was unconstitutional, as the President could not dissolve an assembly that had not yet been convened – not least on the basis of a governor's report that was grounded in mere suspicions of horse-trading.

One of the early skirmishes involved the issue of whether, as the petitioners contended, the court could issue notice to the governor seeking his participation in the proceedings. The court concluded that it could not do so (since Article 361 of the Constitution states that the governor cannot be held answerable to a court for the exercise of his powers), but that it could nevertheless scrutinize his reports and the proclamation issued by the President. According to the Supreme Court, the governor enjoyed immunity, but his decisions and reports did not. President Kalam keenly followed the proceedings in the Supreme Court, and was not pleased with the way his decision was presented to the court.[7] Kalam noted that the court had not been fully apprised of his discussions with the government, and the sequence of events that had taken place when he was in Moscow.

This case offered a good example of how the courts often struggle to keep up with the pace of politics. On 3 September 2005, the Election Commission announced dates for fresh elections in Bihar. Elections would take place in four phases, with voting to commence on 18 October and to conclude on 19 November. By that stage, though the writ petitions had been filed, the hearing at the Supreme Court had not even begun. This presented a quandary for the court. If it decided that the dissolution of the assembly was unconstitutional, what remedy could it offer the petitioners if the next elections were already under way or concluded? Could it reconstitute the dissolved assembly despite the people's fresh mandate and the time and money spent on the next elections? Matters would be more complicated if the fresh mandate was vastly different from the mandate within the dissolved assembly, as the court would effectively be reinstating a government that had lost its popular legitimacy.

Ultimately, the Supreme Court swiftly concluded the hearing by 29 September 2005, over a period of six days. Political parties were left in suspense on the last day of the hearing, as the bench observed, 'We want to allay impressions and conjectures and surmises about the time when the verdict would be delivered. Considering the nature of the cases, we will not be able to give judgment before October 18. We may come out with a short judgment, if necessary, before 18 October and the detailed judgment will follow. Otherwise, there would be one main judgment.'[8] This was interpreted as suggesting that the court would pronounce its decision early if the dissolution was held unconstitutional, and would do so later if the dissolution was upheld.

As it happened, the Supreme Court issued a brief order one week later, the last day before the court closed for the Dussehra break, with detailed reasons to follow. The timing of the decision aligned with the expected outcome. The court held that the President's proclamation dissolving the Bihar Assembly was unconstitutional. However, more surprising than the outcome was the remedy. Despite the unconstitutionality of the proclamation, the court chose not to reinstate the assembly since election preparations were afoot. As the next elections had already been planned and considerable resources had been expended, no legal remedy was made available to those that filed the proceedings. (One op-ed at the time described this as akin to the court issuing a 'conviction without a sentence'.[9]) However, what the BJP and the JDU were denied in terms of legal remedies was compensated through the political traction that they secured upon the court's endorsement of their position. Conversely, the court's decision was seen as a rebuke to the governor and the President, and by implication, the UPA government.

As would have been expected, the NDA demanded the removal or resignation of Governor Buta Singh following the court's decision. Four days after the court's decision, Singh travelled to Delhi (ostensibly on a personal trip to visit ailing relatives). However, there was widespread speculation that Singh used the opportunity to meet with leaders from the UPA government and the Congress party to consider an appropriate response to the court's decision. Media reports suggested that the leadership seriously considered asking the governor to resign.[10] However, following deliberations, it was determined that Buta Singh would not be asked to resign and would continue in office at least until the Supreme Court issued the detailed reasons for its decision. The Congress leadership arrived at this conclusion after considering the possibility of Singh's resignation being perceived as an admission of responsibility, which would not bode well for the party's fortunes in the forthcoming elections in Bihar.[11]

The people of Bihar delivered a more decisive verdict in the election of October–November 2005. The JDU and the BJP collectively gained fifty-one additional seats from their performance in the February elections, most of which were at the expense of the RJD and the LJP. This gave the NDA a comfortable majority in the assembly.

Governor Singh had to 'swallow his pride'[12] and invite the NDA to form the government. Nitish Kumar was sworn in as chief minister. Governor Singh's position remained vulnerable to any criticism that could be forthcoming from the Supreme Court's reasoned decision.

The court's reasoned decision came about two months later, on 24 January 2006, two days before Republic Day. It was argued on behalf of the four MLAs that the President lacked the authority to dissolve the assembly in circumstances where the first meeting of the assembly had not yet taken place. The logic of the argument was simple – it is impossible to dissolve an assembly that has not yet come into existence. Chief Justice Sabharwal rejected this argument on the basis that no provision of the Constitution stipulated that an assembly could only be dissolved after its first meeting. The argument would also yield unintended consequences, for it could imply that there would be a constitutional stalemate in the event that no political party came forward to stake a claim to the government following an election. If no political party staked a claim to form the government, the assembly could not be convened, and therefore could also not be dissolved to enable fresh elections to be called.

While the court rejected the argument that the President could *never* dissolve a legislative assembly before its first meeting, it held that the decision to dissolve the assembly was unconstitutional in that instance. The dissolution was based exclusively on Governor Buta Singh's reports. The governor lacked any credible material in support of his conclusion that an attempt was being made to win over opposition MLAs through bribes and other allurements. Chief Justice Sabharwal also observed that the governor's primary task was simply to ascertain whether a political party or alliance could form a stable government. There were well-established conventions as to the pecking order the governor should follow in inviting parties or alliances to stake a claim to form the government when a single party did not secure an absolute majority. For example, the largest pre-poll alliance would take priority, followed by the single largest party, thereafter followed by the largest post-poll alliance. The governor's role, according to the chief justice, was not to ensure good governance or promote transparency in politics. Those were tasks that were better performed by the opposition and the electorate than the governor.

The court also made some damning remarks about the role of the governor through this episode. According to the chief justice, the governor misled the council of ministers, resulting in them advising the President to issue a proclamation dissolving the assembly. The presidential proclamation could not be justified on the 'suspicion, whims and fancies of the Governor'.[13] The court did not stop with the conduct of the governor, but went as far as imputing ulterior motives: 'The action of the governor was a mere pretence, the real object being to keep away a political party from staking a claim to form the government.'[14]

The Supreme Court's decision was not unanimous, with two of the five judges on the panel dissenting from the majority view. According to Justice Pasayat, the governor was not obliged to remain a silent spectator in the face of attempts to form a government through dishonest means. He would have granted a wide margin of discretion to the governor: 'However suspicious [the] conduct of the governor may be, and even if it is accepted that he had acted in hot haste it cannot be a ground to term his action as extraneous.'[15] For Justice Balakrishnan (who would later become chief justice), a government formed by foul means could hardly be described as a democratically elected government. In his view, the majority's decision was antithetical to, rather than in furtherance of, democratic values.

The Supreme Court's decision provoked serious deliberations within the Congress party and the UPA government. Any ideas of filing a petition in the court seeking a review of its decision were shot down on the basis that there was a risk the court would further reprimand the governor, or worse still, the government. Damage control was the order of the day. Given the court's remarks about the role of the governor, Buta Singh's position appeared untenable. Widespread expectations were that he would either resign or be removed by the government.

However, Singh remained obdurate in the initial moments following the decision. When asked about his intentions following the court's decision, Singh indicated that he would take the Republic Day salute in Patna.[16] The UPA government was increasingly concerned that if it attempted to remove him or compel him to resign, there was a risk that he would turn against the government. Singh 'knew too much', and there was 'no way of knowing what Singh could do, or how he could be controlled after demitting office'.[17] It had long been suspected that the RJD (which was a member of the UPA) had pressured the UPA government to dissolve the assembly on the eve of an attempt to form the state government. The UPA government hardly wanted this confirmed in excruciating detail by one of the protagonists of this episode. Much to the relief of the government, Singh resigned after taking the Republic Day salute on 26 January 2006.

While the Supreme Court did not go so far as to directly censure President Kalam, there were murmurs as to whether he would accept moral responsibility for what was, in the final analysis, a judgement striking down his proclamation dissolving the Bihar Assembly.

Kalam seriously contemplated resigning, going as far as discussing his resignation with his brother and his close advisers.[18] He even kept a letter of resignation ready. It was Prime Minister Manmohan Singh who persuaded the President not to resign, stating that it could result in the UPA government itself toppling.[19] A governor and a state government were casualties during this episode. The President – in particular, among India's most respected and popular Presidents – escaped only narrowly.

Part 2

Gender

Part 2

Gender

4

Tukaram
v
State of Maharashtra

In a nation where social attitudes towards rape and other violent crimes against women focus on the victim rather than the perpetrator, very rarely do instances of such crimes galvanize public opinion and drive reform. One such instance was in 2012, when the rape of 'Nirbhaya' in a moving bus on the streets of Delhi prompted widespread protests and amendments to the criminal law. Four decades before Nirbhaya, it was Mathura. To describe the rape of Mathura committed by a couple of men as an outrageous crime is an oversimplification. Rather, the Mathura case involved a colossal failure of public institutions – including not just the police and the lower judiciary, but also the Supreme Court.

~

Desaiganj is a town about 130 kilometres southeast of Nagpur, in the state of Maharashtra. Bordering Chhattisgarh, it now lies at the heart of the Naxal belt. It was home to Mathura, an Adivasi teenager. Although her precise age was not known at the time, she was thought to be between fourteen and sixteen.

Mathura was a child of difficult personal circumstances. She was an orphan, and lived with her brother, Gama. Mathura and Gama worked as physical labourers. She often visited Nunshi and Laxman's home for work. During the course of these visits, Mathura developed a relationship with, and ultimately married, Nunshi's nephew Ashok. Possibly because he didn't accept the relationship, in March 1972 Gama decided to file a police complaint at the Desaiganj police station claiming that Mathura had been kidnapped by Ashok, Nunshi and Laxman.

Head Constable Baburao recorded the complaint, and instructed that Mathura and her husband Ashok, together with Nunshi and her husband Laxman, be brought to the police station. The four of them arrived at the police station by 9 p.m. on Sunday, 26 March 1972. By about 10.30 p.m., the police had finished taking the statements of Mathura and Ashok. Baburao's dinner was getting delayed. He decided to call it a night, permitting those at the police station to leave, and instructing Gama to return with documents demonstrating Mathura's date of birth.

As those at the police station proceeded to leave, two constables – Ganpat and Tukaram – requested Mathura to wait inside the station and asked the others to leave. When Mathura was inside, the lights of the police station were switched off and the main door locked. Ganpat took Mathura to the latrine towards the back of the police station and removed her undergarments. Thereafter, he dragged Mathura to a veranda, also towards the back of the building, and raped her. Tukaram then approached Mathura and also attempted to rape her. But he was so intoxicated that he was unable to do so.

With the lights having been switched off, the main door locked, and no sign of Mathura, those that were still waiting outside the police station realized that something was amiss. Nunshi shouted out for Mathura, but there was no response. By this time, a crowd had gathered around the police station. Tukaram was the first to emerge, and told Nunshi that Mathura had already left. Mathura appeared shortly thereafter, and recounted the events at the police station to Nunshi and Gama. Little did Mathura and those who cared for her know that the worst of her ordeal was not yet over. In fact, in many ways, it was only just beginning. All instrumentalities of the state would now conspire to revictimize Mathura repeatedly over a number of years. The establishment would hold *her* – rather than Ganpat and Tukaram – responsible for the rape.

As word about the incident at Desaiganj police station spread, the crowd gathered there began to grow increasingly agitated. Head Constable Baburao was contacted as the crowds threatened to burn down the police station. He persuaded the crowd to disperse and registered an FIR. Mathura was left with no alternative but to give a detailed statement to the male colleague of the men who had raped and assaulted her.

She was examined by a doctor nearly twenty-four hours after the incident. The method of medical examination reeked of social prejudices by focusing attention on the sexual history of the victim. Doctors at the time conducted the 'two-finger' test on rape victims. The test postulated that inserting two fingers into the vagina would enable doctors to determine the 'laxity' of the vagina, and whether the hymen had already been ruptured. The implication of the vagina admitting two fingers relatively easily was twofold – first, that the woman was not a virgin and had been sexually active and second, that it was more likely than not that penetration had taken place.

After the case was filed and investigations completed, the case arose for decision before the sessions judge at Chandrapur, a town about 150 kilometres southwest of Desaiganj. The fact that the case reached this stage was an achievement in and of itself. Many women would not have had the resolve to file a complaint in the first place. Those that did would be pressured into withdrawing it once filed. But not Mathura. Mathura and the witnesses for the prosecution commuted to Chandrapur by bus during the trial.[1] Judgement day at the sessions court arrived on 1 June 1974, just over two years after the incident.

The judgement of the sessions court reaffirmed the beliefs of those thousands of women who chose not to pursue proceedings against their assailants. Ganpat and Tukaram were both acquitted, but what would have stung far more are the terms on which the judge acquitted them. Mathura was described as a 'shocking liar', whose testimony was 'riddled with falsehood and improbabilities'. The medical examination and the fact that there were no signs of a physical struggle, resistance, screams or protest weighed heavily on the judge's mind. This led the judge to conclude that the only part of Mathura's account that he was willing to believe was that 'she had sexual intercourse', 'in all probability' with Ganpat.

The sessions court judge proceeded to reconstruct the events that took place that night in an extraordinary way. In the court's view, Mathura had chosen to engage in consensual sexual intercourse with Ganpat. The doctor's testimony confirmed that she was 'habituated to sexual intercourse' – the logic being that a woman who had had

71

sex previously was more likely to consent to having sex in the future, even if with a complete stranger in unfamiliar territory. That still begged the important question of why Mathura would allege rape in circumstances where she engaged in consensual sexual intercourse. The court's answer to this question was that Mathura 'invented the story of rape' in order to 'sound virtuous'. After all, the crowd gathered outside the police station 'included her lover Ashok' as well as her employer Nunshi, who was 'angry' and would have suspected 'something fishy'.

With the stroke of a pen, Mathura was transformed into a woman whose insatiable desire for sex led her to have consensual intercourse with a constable at a police station in the middle of the night, with her family and friends waiting outside. In the court's opinion, she then devised a rape allegation in order to protect her 'honour'. Other important pieces of evidence were cast aside based on ludicrous assumptions. Stains on Mathura's pyjamas were accounted for as having likely been caused by Ashok – the two were, after all, 'very much in love'. The court noted that Ganpat himself was 'no novice', and therefore stains on his pyjamas could have arisen from other previous sexual encounters.

The case then proceeded to the Nagpur bench of the Bombay High Court. Over four years had now elapsed since the incident at Desaiganj police station. In October

1976, the high court took a different view of the facts and evidence. It found Mathura's account credible, and noted that there was a difference between consent and 'passive submission'. The defendants were strangers and Mathura was at the police station in the context of a complaint filed by her brother. The power dynamics between them were heavily skewed in favour of Ganpat and Tukaram, not only because they were officers of the state but also because they were specifically investigating a case involving Mathura. Mathura alleged rape immediately upon emerging from the police station. All of the surrounding circumstances indicated that this may have been an instance of passive submission, but certainly was not consent: '[M]ere passive or helpless surrender of the body and its resignation to the other's lust induced by threats or fear cannot be equated with the desire or will.'[2]

The high court convicted Ganpat of rape and Tukaram of 'outraging the modesty of a woman', and sentenced them to rigorous imprisonment for terms of five years and one year respectively. Although the court could have imposed sentences of twice that length on each of them, many other aspects of its decision were progressive and carefully considered. The court took account of the imbalance of power between the parties. It acknowledged that being in the unlawful custody of the police, Mathura was in an inherently difficult position. Finally, it served as a reminder that consent was a more sophisticated concept than the failure to resist, scream or protest.

Unfortunately, the high court's judgement would not stand for long. Ganpat and Tukaram appealed against their sentences. About two years after the high court judgement, in 1978, three judges of the Supreme Court made their decision in the appeal. The Supreme Court reverted to the sessions court's reasoning that the 'absence of injuries implies consent'.[3] Although the Supreme Court did not describe Mathura as a 'shocking liar' in those many words, it may as well have done so. According to the court, the fact that Mathura bore no injury marks indicated that what took place within the police station was a 'peaceful affair', and that Mathura's story was 'all false'.[4]

The Supreme Court also rejected the high court's reasoning that Mathura's case may have involved passive submission, but was not consent. The court observed that when Mathura was prevented from leaving the police station, she did not raise an alarm despite the presence of Gama, Ashok and Nunshi. She simply should not have 'meekly' followed Ganpat, allowing him to satisfy his 'lust in full'.[5] She could not have been 'so overawed' that she made no attempt to resist. The clear message was that anything other than a 'no' accompanied by violent resistance – no matter how dangerous – would be construed as a 'yes'.

Under the criminal law as it existed at the time, sexual intercourse with a woman constituted 'rape' when it was against her will or without her consent. Rape also included circumstances where intercourse took place with her consent where that consent was induced through fear of death or injury. The Supreme Court focused on this definition of rape, and observed that there was no evidence that Mathura consented under a fear of death or injury. Instead of ascertaining whether Mathura consented in the first place (as the high court did), the Supreme Court *assumed* that Mathura consented and worked backwards from that assumption. With that fundamentally different starting point, the court acquitted Ganpat.

Tukaram met with a similar fate. The court described Mathura's allegations against him as 'wholly unproved'. Citing inconsistencies in her story, the court proposed 'not to take the girl at her word'. After all, where was 'the assurance that her word is truthful in relation to what she now says about Tukaram'? Ganpat's and Tukaram's appeals were upheld, with Mathura's courageous quest for justice going in vain.

As it happened, the Supreme Court was engaged in the exercise of rehabilitating its image as a sentinel of human rights at the time, following its loss of face during the Emergency. Only a few months before the Mathura case, the court held in a celebrated judgement that a procedure established by law which derogates from the fundamental right to life under the Constitution must be 'fair, just and reasonable, not fanciful, oppressive or arbitrary'.[6] About a month before the judgement, the court held in another case that providing free legal aid to prisoners was the 'State's duty and not government charity'.[7] These lofty exhortations about protecting rights did not seem to extend to Mathura.

The Supreme Court's judgement in the Mathura case garnered little attention when it was first pronounced in September 1978. Almost exactly a year after the Supreme Court's judgement, four academics – three from the University of Delhi and one from the University of Pune – wrote an open letter to the chief justice of India, Justice Y.V. Chandrachud, criticizing the decision.[8] The letter written by Upendra Baxi, Vasudha Dhagamwar, Raghunath Kelkar and Lotika Sarkar was a brief, but decisive, inquisition of all aspects of the court's decision. The academics observed that the court's judgement overlooked important factual considerations: that the rape arose from Mathura's wrongful confinement by the police and that Tukaram was intoxicated on duty. They also noted the court's mistaken understanding of the law on rape: '[T]here is a clear difference in law, and common sense, between "submission" and "consent". Consent involves submission; but the converse is not necessarily true.' Perhaps most importantly, they highlighted that the decision was based on chauvinistic assumptions. Mathura's sexual history demonstrated that she was likely to have consented; Ganpat's sexual history was considered evidence of the absence of rape: '[W]hy this double standard? Ganpat's sexual habits give him the benefit of doubt of having raped Mathura; her sexual habits make the Court disbelieve the story of the rape altogether.'

The letter concluded with a plea to have Mathura's case reheard at the Supreme Court by a larger panel of judges, possibly even the whole court. The letter offered the following justification for what the authors themselves described as a 'startlingly unconventional, and even a naive suggestion':

[N]othing short of protection of human rights and constitutionalism is at stake . . . Maybe on re-examination Ganpat and Tukaram may stand acquitted for better reasons than those now available. But what matters is a search for liberation from the colonial and male-dominated notions of what may constitute the element of consent, and the burden of proof, for rape which affect many Mathuras on the Indian countryside.[9]

The open letter did not manage to capture attention in the weeks after it was sent. One of its authors noted that *Dawn*, a newspaper based in Pakistan, was first among the mainstream media to publish a report based on the letter. The news spread in India quite swiftly thereafter, and Mathura's case became part of the public consciousness within months. Wider awareness about the court's decision and the injustice meted out to Mathura sparked protests across the country. The protests took many forms, including demonstrations, speeches, discussions, poster campaigns, plays and skits. They were organized across cities, towns and villages – from Delhi to Kolhapur, Hyderabad to Belgaum, and Pune to Palghar.[10]

A public meeting was organized in Bombay on 25 February 1980 to discuss legal, political and social aspects of rape. Ahead of that meeting, street plays were performed and songs sung on women's liberation. A ten-minute Hindi play was performed depicting how female complainants are revictimized when filing a complaint at a police station. The meeting included broad-based discussions on rape, many of them involving keen audience participation. Karate and judo sessions were held to improve women's self-defence capabilities.[11] Marches and demonstrations were organized about two weeks later, on International Women's Day.[12]

A report from March 1980 described a protest

by Adivasi women in Talasari, a town close to the Maharashtra–Gujarat border, which extended beyond rape to the socio-economic conditions of women:

> 1500 women marched to the Tahsildar's office and the police station . . . They demanded the reopening of the Mathura case . . . they spoke about rape in their own lives, by policemen, contractors, moneylenders and shopkeepers. Others spoke about the evils of alcoholism which they maintain had been introduced by the moneylenders and landlords. Some spoke on rising prices, the right to work, and the corruption in the employment guarantee scheme.[13]

The mobilization of women's groups in the aftermath of Mathura's case was unprecedented. Previously isolated women's groups drew strength from collective protests cutting across ideologies. As one editorial written ten years later put it: 'The protest was widespread, it drew women across party lines and it was unanimous.'[14] Several women's rights groups were established. This included the Forum Against Rape (later rechristened the Forum Against Oppression of Women), which circulated leaflets and circulars in different parts of the country in an attempt to gather support for the protests. One of the forum's leaflets was entitled 'Isn't It Time We

Looked Rape in the Face?' It included several powerful exhortations urging society to escape the squeamishness about rape:

> Isn't it time we accepted that it [rape] does occur, all the time, everywhere? Accept that all women are potential victims – be they young or old, attractive or plain, 'nice' or 'not nice', rich or poor?

> The Mathuras of the country are doubly oppressed, they are women and they belong to an already oppressed section in a nation where justice is the privilege of a few.

> [Y]ou don't have to be raped to realize what you're up against. Don't you know it already? Doesn't every woman know it?

> Will you be one of the 800 cases reported in Bombay in one year and have the courage to say 'I was raped'? Or will you be one of the 8,000 others, for to every reported rape there are 10–12 unreported ones?[15]

Women's and students' organizations in Delhi, including the National Federation of Indian Women, Stree Sangharsh, the Delhi University Students' Union and the Indraprastha College Women's Committee, combined to form the Joint Action Committee Against

Rape and Sexual Harassment. They published a ten-point memorandum seeking 'decisive and immediate' steps in the aftermath of the Mathura case.[16] This included the reopening of the Mathura case, a suspension and departmental inquiry against Tukaram and Ganpat, amending the rape law to exclude evidence concerning a woman's past sexual history, harsher sentences in rape cases and special courts for speedy trials and decisions.

The protests were directed towards two avenues. The first was the Supreme Court, which was asked to reopen the Mathura case. Review petitions filed by several organizations were dismissed on the basis that they lacked the standing to do so as third parties to the case. The court was nevertheless conscious that its decision in the Mathura case damaged its reputation in respect of women's rights. It therefore formulated a 'face saving measure' in a case that arose shortly thereafter.[17] In determining whether corroborating evidence (in addition to the evidence of the victim) was required in cases involving sexual offences, the Supreme Court answered in the negative. This would have been a welcome decision for women's rights groups, had it not been for the court's justification – which reinforced (rather than challenged) the prejudices underpinning the Mathura judgement. The court reasoned its decision on the basis that Indian women were different from women in the 'Western World', and were unlikely to concoct an allegation of sexual assault.[18] Women in the West could be driven by economic motives, 'psychological neurosis', vengeance or jealousy to fabricate allegations. An Indian woman, conscious of the 'danger of being osctracised', the 'reflect[tion] on her chastity' and other factors, was unlikely to do so.[19]

The second avenue was to secure reforms in the criminal law through the government and Parliament. To be clear, the Supreme Court's decision was plainly wrong on the law as it stood at the time. Nevertheless, several aspects of the law tilted the scales in favour of the defendants. The identity of rape complainants was neither protected nor anonymized. The law did not specifically address rape in custodial situations. There were no restrictions on the use of a woman's sexual history in evidence.

Soon after the general elections of 1980, the Congress government asked the Law Commission to study the law on rape and sexual assault of women. The government was under severe public pressure, and conveyed this clearly to the Law Commission in its letter dated 27 March 1980.[20] The letter was especially frank, for its focus was on the 'considerable amount of discussion in the Press and in other forums' and 'strong public opinion' on the law of rape, rather than on the inherent importance of addressing the inadequacies of the law.[21] Having been asked to give this study 'top most priority',[22] the Law

Commission worked at breakneck speed, producing a forty-two page report within a few weeks.[23]

The Law Commission's report suggested several far-reaching amendments to the law. Most significant among them was the recommendation that in a situation where sexual intercourse is established and the woman has stated in her evidence that she did not consent, courts should presume that a woman did not consent. It would then be the defendant's responsibility to dislodge that presumption based on evidence. According to the Law Commission, consent was not sufficient in and of itself – that consent had to be 'free and voluntary'. The Commission also recommended increasing the minimum age of consent from sixteen to eighteen – meaning that sex with a female below that age would be treated as rape. It was averse to the idea of prescribing a minimum sentence of imprisonment for rape, on the basis that this was inconsistent with modern penology.

After eleven years, three judgements, dozens of protests and a Law Commission report, the Mathura case ultimately prompted legislative amendments. However, the debates leading up to these amendments were marked by patriarchy and 'structured by the discourse of shame and stigma'.[24] One MP from the Congress party observed that: '[S]ome girls are very clever and are the agents of police. These days it's the world of politics, police can falsely accuse any-one it wants on charge of rape ... You have written here that the girl's past history will not be asked, then how will you come to know about the girl?' Another from the Communist Party of India was not far behind: 'A rape victim is practically given the same status as a prostitute. She bears a stigma in the eyes of the society. She has to hide herself. She cannot openly say what's happened to her.'[25] And still another MP expressed a similar sentiment in the following words: 'Once a lady is raped, not only is she not acceptable by society, but also she is not acceptable by the parents ... ultimately she has to live a life of a prostitute.'[26]

Perhaps unsurprisingly, then, the final product was significant but somewhat underwhelming. Many of the Law Commission's recommendations were disregarded. Parliament did not go so far as to presume a lack of consent when the complainant said she did not consent. Instead, it enacted special provisions to address custodial situations. Where a woman in police custody claimed that she did not consent, the courts would now have to presume that she did not consent. Provisions were also introduced to address custodial situations that did not meet the legal definition of rape. Where a public servant took advantage of his official position to have sex with a woman in his custody, he would now be liable to imprisonment of up to five years even in the absence of any evidence of rape. A similar provision was introduced in respect of superintendents of jails, remand homes and shelters.

The Law Commission's recommendation to avoid prescribing a minimum sentence of imprisonment for rape was disregarded. The minimum sentence for rape was now set at seven years in most instances, and ten years in some others – with the maximum sentence being life imprisonment. Parliament also attempted to address the identification and revictimization of rape victims following the offence. It was now a criminal offence to disclose the identity of the rape victim without her consent. There were some discernible omissions from the debates leading up to the legislative reform and the amendments themselves – the conversation focused on rape in custodial situations, ignoring the equally important issue of rape within the four walls of the home.

All the while, even as the rape of an Adivasi child galvanized the women's movement and produced legislative reforms, Mathura herself remained on the sidelines. She is reported to have moved to a different village, remarried and started a family. All those years ago, Mathura did what most other women of her time would not have had the resolve to do for fear of a social backlash, police apathy, judicial delays and a host of other reasons. She filed a rape complaint and followed it through to its logical conclusion. The Supreme Court – famously described at the time as the 'last resort for the oppressed and bewildered'[27] – failed her.

5

R.D. Bajaj
v
K.P.S. Gill

On Wednesday, 27 July 2005, senior civil servant Rupan Deol Bajaj's quest for justice finally came to a close. The Supreme Court confirmed the conviction of K.P.S. Gill, the 'supercop' who ended the militancy and Khalistan separatist movement in Punjab, for slapping her on the bottom at a party in 1988. This was the culmination of a legal process that was neither swift nor easy. It involved no less than eight judgements over a period of seventeen years; decisions by several senior judges; complaints *to* bureaucrats, *by* bureaucrats, *against* bureaucrats; and claims of government secrecy and privilege. In the time that the case meandered from one court to the next,

India had seen eighteen chief justices and nine prime ministers. And yet, the legacy of this case remained highly contested.

~

On 18 July 1988, Surrinder Lal Kapur – an IAS officer and a senior bureaucrat in the Punjab government – hosted a dinner party at his home in Sector 16, Chandigarh. Kapur was known for throwing 'lively parties', with an abundance of alcohol, that were frequented by the city's elites.[1] This one was no different, with a guest list that included twenty-five of the most senior bureaucrats, police officers and lawyers in the city, many of whom were accompanied by their spouses. The joint director of the Intelligence Bureau (IB), the inspector general of the Chandigarh Police and the advocate general of Punjab were all present that evening. In the recent past, the government of Punjab had developed a strategy of cultivating the media for better press, in order to secure more favourable coverage of its response to the separatist movement.[2] In step with this strategy, Kapur had also invited a group of journalists (including from the *Hindustan Times*, the *Indian Express*, the Press Trust of India and *India Today*) to the party.

Among the most high-profile attendees that evening

was K.P.S. Gill, director general of the Punjab Police. Gill had acquired the reputation of being an uncompromising and ruthless police officer, and was tasked with addressing the widespread violence in the state. As one scholar noted, Gill 'offered the terrorists a stark choice: they could either die for their idea of God, or live for themselves. There was no third option.'[3] He had just come off a resounding success in Operation Black Thunder, in which a large group of terrorists was cleared from the Golden Temple in Amritsar.

Rupan Deol Bajaj and her husband B.R. Bajaj, both senior IAS officers of the Punjab cadre, arrived at the Kapur residence at about 9 p.m. The guests were seated in the lawn at the back of the house. As was customary, cane chairs were arranged to form two semicircles facing one another – the men would sit in one of the semicircles and the women in the other. About an hour later, Gill walked over to the women's semicircle, and occupied a vacant chair about five to six seats away from Mrs Bajaj. Many of the women seated around Gill happened to be rising from their seats and entering the house around that time. Gill called out to Bajaj, and asked her to sit on the vacant chair next to him. He pulled the chair closer to his as Bajaj was about to sit down. Bajaj pulled the chair back to its original position, but Gill repeated the gesture. Realizing that 'something was very wrong',[4]

Bajaj returned to her original seat between two women in the semicircle.

A few minutes later, Gill approached and stood directly in front of Bajaj – so close that his legs were about four inches from her knees. Crooking his finger, he demanded that she stand up and come along with him. By this time, the other women in the semicircle were 'shocked and speechless'.[5] Bajaj responded, 'Mr Gill, how dare you! You are behaving in an obnoxious manner, go away from here.'[6] When Gill persisted with his request, Bajaj pulled her chair back, creating enough room to exit between her chair and the chair of one of the women sitting next to her (who was Mrs Bijlani, the wife of the managing director of a company that manufactured machinery). As Bajaj rose from her chair and turned to leave, Gill slapped her on the bottom.

Bajaj was furious and determined not to let this pass. Her initial response was to approach her host Kapur, who was standing on a paved platform adjacent to the lawn. Unrepentant, Gill followed Bajaj on her way to speak to Kapur. She told Kapur that Gill was not fit for decent company, that he had misbehaved with her, and that he had gone to the extent of hitting her. Together with another guest, Kapur then physically escorted Gill away from the lawn and into the house. Bajaj also narrated the incident to G.C. Pathak, the joint director of the IB, who was standing by. Pathak promised that he had made a note of this incident and would report it to the relevant authorities within the central government.

Bajaj was congratulated by the other women for her fortitude in dealing with Gill's conduct. When she informed her husband about what had happened, his instinct was to pursue Gill at that moment. She restrained him from doing so, particularly since members of the press were present. Bajaj later recounted that as they were leaving, she overheard one of the other guests deplore Gill's behaviour from that evening: 'This man made me feel like vomiting.'[7] Even as many of the guests left the party with a bad taste in their mouth, most of them would have expected that what happened at the Kapur residence would stay in the Kapur residence. There was a tacit understanding that these elite gatherings were meant to be closed to the outside world, misbehaviour or not.

Bajaj had other ideas. She was determined on seeing Gill reprimanded for his misconduct. Since they were both members of the civil service, Bajaj thought that disciplinary action against Gill by the government (rather than criminal proceedings) would be the swiftest and most effective response. She approached R.P. Ojha, chief secretary of Punjab and 'blue eyed boy'[8] to Governor S.S. Ray. Ojha's response was unsympathetic: 'Rupan, these things keep happening. You are not diminished.

Consider yourself lucky, it could have been worse . . .'[9]
She then approached Julio Ribeiro, Gill's predecessor as
director general of the Punjab Police.[10] Ribeiro was now
adviser to the governor. He took note as Bajaj recounted
the events of that evening. He promised to share a draft
of the note with her before sending it to the governor, to
enable Bajaj to confirm that it was accurate. As it happens,
the report was sent to the governor the next day without
the draft being shared with Bajaj.

When Bajaj met with the secretary to Governor Ray
seeking an appointment with the governor, the secretary
informed her that Ribeiro had already sent his report
to the governor. The governor was understood to have
summoned Gill and privately censured him for his
conduct.[11] Governor Ray made a proposal that Bajaj
considered entirely unsatisfactory: that Gill would be
debarred from attending dinner parties after 8.30 p.m.,
and that he would apologize to her in private. Bajaj
even approached the secretary in Prime Minister Rajiv
Gandhi's office, but this was to no avail. Until then, the
media – including the journalists present at the Kapur
party – had chosen to abide by unwritten norms and
not report the story. A special correspondent from the
Indian Post, a Bombay-based newspaper, decided to break
the silence.[12] What was up to then known only among
the elite in Chandigarh (and perhaps to some extent,

in Delhi) was now disseminated across the country. A
senior IAS officer had accused national hero K.P.S. Gill
of sexually harassing her at a dinner party.

By then, over eleven days had passed since the party
at the Kapur residence. Seeking justice through an
administrative remedy had proven futile. Bajaj decided
to file a police complaint. She lodged a complaint with
the inspector general of the Chandigarh Police, who, as
it happened, had also been at the party. In her complaint,
Bajaj alleged that Gill committed several offences under
the Indian Penal Code (IPC). These included crimes under
Section 354 (the use of criminal force against a woman
with an intention to 'outrage her modesty') and Section
509 (speech, sounds or gestures intended to insult the
'modesty of any woman'). Both offences were punishable
with a fine and/or a sentence of imprisonment of up to
two years (for Section 354) and one year (for Section 509).

If it took a few days for Bajaj to learn that it would
be difficult to secure any meaningful administrative
or disciplinary action against Gill, it took only a few
moments for her to realize that criminal conviction
would be even harder. The inspector general registered
her complaint, gave Bajaj a receipt and sealed a hard copy
of the complaint in an envelope, rather than placing it in
the file of complaints. On being asked by Bajaj why the
complaint was being placed in a sealed envelope, he said

that his duty was only to register the complaint: 'What I do with it after that is entirely up to me.'[13] He told Bajaj that he would not actively investigate the complaint without a court order.

Unsurprisingly, the police investigation went nowhere as weeks and months passed after the complaint was filed. The Bajajs got wind of the fact that the police were preparing to close the investigation because – despite there being so many eyewitnesses to the incident – no corroborating evidence was available, as none of the eyewitnesses were forthcoming. It is unlikely that the eyewitnesses to the incident would have wanted to be involved in a 'police case', not least against a person as powerful as Gill. This prompted Mr Bajaj to file a separate complaint with the chief judicial magistrate about four months after the party at the Kapur residence. In his complaint, Mr Bajaj alleged that as a result of Gill's position, a fair and impartial investigation of the case had not taken place. The police had neither arrested Gill, nor undertaken any meaningful investigation following Mrs Bajaj's complaint. To provide evidence in support of his complaint, Mr Bajaj asked the magistrate to summon the report sent by Ribeiro to the governor, as well as an order passed by the governor a few days thereafter (which included the injunction on Gill attending dinner parties after 8.30 p.m.). Parts of Ribeiro's report were already alleged to have been leaked to the press, including his prognosis that Gill was 'in the habit of getting drunk and misbehaving with women'.[14]

The request for disclosure of the reports of the governor and his adviser yielded an unexpected battle. The government of Punjab staunchly opposed the disclosure of these reports, on the basis that they were privileged and concerned affairs of the state. An affidavit filed by Chief Secretary Ojha stated that the disclosure of the reports would 'hamper the proper functioning of the public service as the officers would in future feel hesitant in expressing their opinions fearlessly in such administrative matters'.[15] The magistrate rejected this claim of privilege stating that the documents did not concern affairs of state, but the conduct of an individual.

The state government challenged the magistrate's decision in the Punjab and Haryana High Court. It had better luck on this occasion. The judge of the high court (coincidentally also a 'Bajaj')[16] held that the reports were protected from disclosure by virtue of Article 163(3) of the Constitution, which stated that no court could inquire into what advice ministers (which would include an adviser such as Ribeiro) tendered to the governor. The court also saw no public interest in the disclosure of these reports, since Ribeiro was not an eyewitness to the incident. For the court, Ribeiro's report would have been no more useful than Mrs Bajaj's own evidence.[17] This time, it was Mr Bajaj that appealed to the Supreme Court against the high court's decision.

In the meantime, Gill had filed a petition asking the Punjab and Haryana High Court to quash the complaints of Mrs and Mr Bajaj. Representing Gill, prominent criminal lawyer K.T.S. Tulsi argued that his client lacked an intention to commit any of the offences alleged. The fact that Mrs Bajaj willingly walked over to Gill to sit next to him when requested, Tulsi argued, demonstrated the absence of any intention to commit a crime (as though consent to have a conversation equates with consent to unwanted physical contact). He also argued that even if Gill had in fact engaged in the conduct alleged, it was so 'slight' that it could not be treated as an offence. The implication of this argument was that the act of slapping a woman on the bottom was so 'slight' that, even though it fell within the letter of the offence, it could not be treated as falling within the scope of the offence.

About ten months from the party at the Kapur residence, the high court held in favour of Gill, quashing the complaints. The high court's reasons were disconcerting. First, there were about fifty other people at the party, and it was 'unnatural and unconscionable' that Gill would 'dare' to commit the offence in their presence.[18] Second, Mrs Bajaj's narrative was inconsistent with the story that she told her host Kapur and fellow guest Pathak, the joint director of the IB, immediately after the incident – that Gill had 'hit her', rather than slapped her on the bottom. The high court ascribed great weight to the fact that she failed to specify 'the part of the body'[19] – as though it was something that Bajaj would want to broadcast and disseminate widely. Third, the court stated that the Bajajs failed to justify the delay of eleven days in filing the police complaint and four months in filing the complaint with the magistrate,[20] ignoring that the police complaint was filed only after administrative measures proved futile, and that the complaint with the magistrate was filed when it became clear that the investigation was not being meaningfully pursued.

At this stage, it appeared that Rupan Deol Bajaj's fight for justice was over. The administration was against her. There were two high court decisions, both issued by her namesake judge, against her. The tide of opinion was squarely against her – in the eyes of the public at large, she was reckless at best, and a devious liar at worst. The most that she had got up to that stage was the offer of a private apology. The prospect of a criminal conviction (or for that matter, any criminal action) against Gill was nowhere on the horizon. Gill was 'the naughty hero who had committed a trivial lapse but who ought to be pardoned on the grounds of state security'.[21] In fact, he was awarded a Padma Shri shortly after the high court's decision. The Bajajs nevertheless played their last card, appealing the decision in the Supreme Court.

Both appeals (the appeal against the decision rejecting the disclosure of Ribeiro's report to the governor and the governor's order, and the appeal against the decision quashing the complaints) were consolidated and considered together by the Supreme Court. It took six years, or to be precise 2,327 days, after the Punjab and Haryana High Court's quashing decision for the Supreme Court to arrive at its decision. KTS continued to represent KPS, but the Bajajs were now represented by senior advocate Indira Jaising. Even at this stage, the lawyer representing the Chandigarh administration suggested that the matter could be put to rest if Gill expressed regret for his conduct.[22] The court chose not to engage with this suggestion, leaving it to the parties to decide whether they wished to compromise in this way.

The two-judge panel of the Supreme Court (comprising Justices Anand and Mukherjee) held that the high court committed a 'gross error of law' in quashing the complaints.[23] Assuming Bajaj's allegations were correct, it was clear that Gill outraged her modesty for the purposes of Sections 354 and 509 of the IPC. His actions were 'not only an affront to the normal sense of feminine decency but also an affront to the dignity' of Bajaj.[24] Gill's suggestion that he lacked any intention to outrage Mrs Bajaj's modesty was rejected. Gill should have known that he would outrage Bajaj's modesty if he slapped her bottom, especially since his actions were 'in the presence of a gathering comprising the elite of the society'.[25] In any event, there was nothing that suggested his actions involved an honest mistake or a slip. The court decisively rejected the argument that his conduct was so 'slight' that it could not be considered an offence, clarifying that 'under no circumstances' could his conduct be considered trivial.[26]

In conclusion, the court took the view that there was sufficient material for the magistrate to take cognizance of the offences, and directed him to conduct the trial of the case. The court made it clear that it did not intend to prejudge the merits of the case, and that the magistrate should make an independent decision. The Supreme Court considered that the appeal over the 'privileged' documents had become otiose by virtue of its decision, and did not decide the questions arising from that appeal. This is because the privileged documents issue arose in the context of Mr Bajaj's complaint. Since the Supreme Court had directed the magistrate to proceed with the trial in respect of Mrs Bajaj's complaint, and

Mr Bajaj's complaint addressed the very same subject matter, his complaint was now redundant. Seven years after the party at the Kapur residence, the trial of K.P.S. Gill was ready to commence.

Despite the Supreme Court's decision, Gill remained relatively confident of his prospects in the trial. He was in transit to Himachal Pradesh to supervise the building of his house on the day of the decision. One news article described him as the 'the picture of relaxation' on the day.[27] His lawyer Tulsi also warned that it was still somewhat early for Bajaj to celebrate victory. This confidence may have flowed from the continuing unwillingness of witnesses to come forward and corroborate Bajaj's account. The best corroborating witness from that evening, Mrs Bijlani, observed, 'There is no question of going to court as witnesses. At the time [when the incident occurred] we gave a statement to the police without thinking. We refused to go to court then and even now, we will not [go].'[28] Public opinion and the press remained firmly in Gill's camp. In her weekly column for the *Indian Express*, journalist Tavleen Singh criticized Bajaj for wasting the Supreme Court's time. In an interview shortly thereafter, she described it as 'quite obscene' that this case could be taken to the highest court of the land, when women in the villages confronted far more pressing concerns.[29]

Given the long delay before the trial could commence, the Supreme Court directed the magistrate to endeavour to conclude the trial within six months. The trial ultimately overshot this time frame by a small margin. Tuesday, 6 August 1996 was D-Day. By now, the Kapur party was faint in the memory – nearly eight years had passed since then. Mrs Bajaj could not bear to be personally present in court when the decision was pronounced. Gill was then president of the Indian Hockey Federation and had retired from the police. His supporters were so confident of his impending victory that, as Bajaj later revealed in an interview to the BBC, the police band was ready outside the court to celebrate his acquittal.[30] Since the state was prosecuting Gill, this yielded the curious result that the police band was standing ready to celebrate the failure of the state prosecution.

Chief Judicial Magistrate Darshan Singh announced that Gill was convicted on both counts. He was sentenced to three months' rigorous imprisonment for 'outraging the modesty' of a woman, and two months' rigorous imprisonment for engaging in speech and gestures intended to 'insult the modesty' of a woman. As the sentences would run concurrently, Gill faced the prospect of spending three months in prison unless he succeeded on appeal. The chief judicial magistrate also imposed fines in the amount of Rs 700 on Gill. After the decision,

Bajaj stated that her stand had been vindicated, while Gill resolved to appeal and pursue his legal remedies until his dignity was restored.[31]

In eight years, judicial opinion about the strength of Bajaj's case had turned, but public opinion had not. The chief judicial magistrate observed in his judgement that Gill could not be treated as any other common citizen, prompting criticism that he had been singled out by virtue of his public profile.[32] The largest English newspapers took editorial positions that were sympathetic to Gill, and in some instances also blamed Bajaj for Gill's indiscretions. Twenty-four hours after the judgement was pronounced, the *Indian Express* took the following editorial line: 'No Indian who is aware of his role in defeating secessionism in Punjab can be happy at Gill's misfortune . . . Unfortunately it is not his humiliation alone; the country too feels a little small today.'[33] Forty-eight hours later, the following appeared in the *Deccan Herald*'s editorial pages: 'It somehow makes the law of the land look grotesquely odd and incongruous that a man who has done signal service to the country by ridding a state of the dread and oppression of terrorism should have to spend five months in jail for a minute's exuberance provoked by the charms of an attractive working woman.'[34] (It should have been 'three months', but that was hardly the most disturbing aspect of the piece.) Seventy-two hours later, it was *The Hindu*'s turn to defend Gill: 'The sentence of three months' rigorous imprisonment . . . although well within his discretion and powers under the relevant section of the Indian Penal Code looks somewhat harsh considering that Gill had an outstanding record as a supercop. If today Punjab is rid of militancy which had taken a heavy toll of human lives in the state a great deal of the credit goes to Gill.'[35]

In the endless cycle of decisions and appeals, it was now the sessions court's turn to determine whether to uphold the judgement of the chief judicial magistrate. (In the judicial hierarchy, appeals from the chief judicial magistrate are to the sessions court, appeals from the sessions court are to the high court, and appeals from the high court are to the Supreme Court.) In January 1998, Sessions Judge Amar Dutt upheld Gill's conviction, but modified his sentence. Gill would no longer need to go to prison, but would remain on probation (an alternative to serving a sentence of imprisonment) upon entering a bond for Rs 20,000 and complying with a creative set of conditions – that he 'be of good behaviour' and appear in court when called upon for a period of three years; that he lead an 'honest and industrious life'; that he abstain from consuming alcohol in public places and at parties; that he remain under the supervision of, and periodically visit, the Delhi chief probation officer for three years; and that he deposit Rs 2,00,000 as compensation to Bajaj and Rs 50,000 towards costs of the legal proceedings.[36]

The sessions judge offered robust reasons for rejecting the arguments presented on behalf of Gill. It was argued that the Bajajs went after Gill driven by political vendetta because Gill had refused to intervene in a CBI inquiry against Mr Bajaj. The sessions judge observed that this argument was entirely unsubstantiated. In response to Gill's argument that her account was unladylike – because any self-respecting lady would have approached her husband in the first instance, before approaching her host Kapur and fellow guest Pathak – the sessions judge held that Mrs Bajaj was an experienced administrator in her own right, and was capable of 'handling this kind of situation independently of her husband'.[37] The judge, however, offered an inexplicable reason for modifying the sentence – that Bajaj was initially content with an apology, but that her 'attitude hardened' with time.[38] Bajaj was in fact always clear that an apology was an unsatisfactory remedy. None of the evidence on the record suggested otherwise.

The sessions judge's decision garnered far less interest in the media and the public response on this occasion was muted.[39] Gill appealed the sessions judge's decision despite the modification of his sentence. And so Gill and Bajaj found themselves in the Punjab and Haryana High

Court for the third time. Justice Bajaj had long retired, and this appeal would be decided by Justice R.L. Anand. On 20 August 1998, the high court also confirmed the conviction of Gill, but further modified the conditions imposed by the sessions judge. The court dropped the conditions that Gill should lead an honest and industrious life and refrain from consuming alcohol in public places, on the basis that they were vague and hard to enforce.[40]

The high court decisively rejected Gill's argument that the prosecution's narrative should be rejected in the absence of corroborating witnesses. However, in arriving at its decision, the court reinforced stereotypes and prejudices. Much of the high court's judgement was directed towards the humiliation associated with what others would think if a woman was sexually harassed, not the trauma that is inherent in being harassed. The judgement offers a catalogue of examples of this: '[An] Indian woman is a symbol of modesty itself. Every part of her body symbolises that she is the specimen of modesty';[41] 'Mrs Bajaj is a woman of the society and in our society still the woman is regarded as a symbol of modesty';[42] 'she cannot accept insult, specially in an elite gathering, otherwise a wrong signal can travel in the elite itself';[43] 'she was humiliated in the presence of others and it was very difficult on her part to swallow it, lest there may be encouragement to the petitioner or lest a wrong signal may travel in the respectable society about her conduct';[44] 'keeping in view the traditions of our country, specially in northern India, no respectable woman would come forward with false allegations';[45] '[t]he alleged act was going to be committed qua a woman, who possibly could not digest the humiliation and the consequences of the act allegedly performed by the petitioner'.[46]

Both Gill and Bajaj decided to appeal against the high court's decision. For Bajaj, Gill had been let off the hook too easily. For Gill, nothing short of exoneration was acceptable. Another long delay between the high court's decision and the Supreme Court's decision followed. The Supreme Court made its decision on 27 July 2005, seventeen years and nine days after the party at the Kapur residence. The final judgement in this case, delivered by Justices Balakrishnan and Srikrishna, was short and succinct. The court rejected the argument that the criminal proceedings were an attempt to malign Gill and observed that his conduct was not befitting that of a top-ranking police officer. Neither Gill's nor Bajaj's final appeals were successful. The high court's decision stood – Gill was convicted, but would not go to prison.

At the Supreme Court, Bajaj made it clear that she had pursued legal proceedings as a matter of principle and had no intention of withdrawing the compensation of Rs 2,00,000 that Gill had been ordered to deposit.

The court therefore directed that the compensation be paid over to a women's rights organization. Even after the Supreme Court's final decision in this case, Gill's lawyer downplayed the judgement as 'academic' since it imposed no practical disqualifications on Gill.[47] Bajaj campaigned, ultimately unsuccessfully, to have Gill's Padma Shri withdrawn.

This case left behind a complex legacy. Throughout the proceedings and thereafter, Bajaj emphasized the broader significance of her case to the women's rights movement. However, Sections 354 and 509 of the IPC were grounded in Victorian conceptions of modesty and honour. These sections typecast women as meek and modest, with crimes arising from the violation of this notion of modesty. The disquieting consequence of framing crimes of sexual assault and harassment in this way was that they appeared to afford protection only to women that retained the quality of modesty. As an upper-class married woman with a powerful husband, and attending a party at which men and women congregated in separate semicircles, Mrs Bajaj matched this description perfectly. As one scholar observed, Bajaj 'called upon a Victorian law to win a remarkably Victorian case, thus enshrining in precedent the image of the working woman as married, modest, surrounded by her stalwart husband and circle of proper "ladies"'.[48] Bajaj presented herself consistent with this narrative. In an interview given shortly after the Supreme Court's final decision, she said, 'If I had not protested then who is supposed to, my class IV employee or peon? I am a role model because of where I am, I just had to.'[49]

Would agricultural labourers or manual scavengers benefit from the same legal protections? Perhaps it would be much too easy to dismiss their claims for the reason that since they had relinquished their 'modesty', there was nothing left to protect. On a separate occasion, Mrs Bajaj said, 'I am not a woman from the roadside. I have had 6,000 men working under me.'[50] It is unthinkable that 'a woman from the roadside', in particular a lower-caste or lower-class woman, would ever secure even the token of justice that Bajaj did.

Part 3
Religion

6

State of Madras
v
Champakam Dorairajan

In less than eighteen months of India becoming a republic, three judges of the Madras High Court and seven judges of the Supreme Court voted to strike down a Madras government order providing for reservations. Prime Minister Nehru was pressured into agreeing to amendments to the Constitution to overturn these decisions and the provisional Parliament (in place until the first general election was held) voted to make those amendments. As two prominent scholars have put it, the 'battle over admissions to higher education is as old as independent India'.[1]

~

In the early years of the twentieth century, there was growing dissatisfaction among non-Brahmins in the Madras Presidency of British India. Brahmins, who comprised a small segment of the population, had disproportionate access to education and government jobs. While they comprised just 3.2 per cent of the population, they occupied 53 per cent of the posts of deputy collector, over 71 per cent of the posts of sub-judge and over 66 per cent of the posts of district munsif.[2] It was in this environment that the South Indian Liberal Federation, otherwise known as the Justice Party, was established as a party 'articulating anti-Brahminism and acting against the ideals of the freedom movement'.[3] The Justice Party considered that the freedom movement was dominated by distinctly Brahminical principles, and preferred to work with the British administration to protect the interests of the non-Brahmins. This resulted in a cleavage among the press too, with the 'nationalist' newspapers sympathetic to the Congress party, and the 'Anglo-Indian' newspapers sympathetic to the Justice Party.

The Justice Party's early achievement was to secure reservation of seats for non-Brahmins in the provincial legislative council, as part of the Montagu–Chelmsford Reforms of 1919. Thereafter, following an extended round of discussions in 1921, the efforts of the Justice Party yielded an order reserving government jobs for non-Brahmins.[4] This order was called the 'Communal G.O.' It prescribed a ratio by which government jobs would be allotted to non-Brahmins, Brahmins, Muslims, Anglo-Indians and Christians. The Communal G.O. met with immediate protests and resistance, including from sections of the Congress party.[5] It could not be put into effect right away.

In 1927, a revised Communal G.O. was passed and implemented.[6] As the influence of the Justice Party waned and the Congress party gained ascendancy in Madras in the 1930s, the Congress made an about-turn from its earlier position, backed the Communal G.O. and made it 'very much its own policy'.[7] The Communal G.O. continued in force even after Independence, although the ratios of allotment changed over time. It was deployed to allocate positions in both government colleges and government jobs. But within weeks of the Constitution coming into force, an aspiring medical student and an aspiring engineering student filed petitions in the Madras High Court challenging the Communal G.O. on the basis that it violated their fundamental rights.

C.R. Srinivasan, a Brahmin, had applied for admission to the Government Engineering College at Guindy. He had completed an intermediate examination at Madras University, scoring 369 out of 450 marks. Srinivasan apprehended that given the small number of seats available at the government engineering colleges (there were just 395 seats across the four colleges in Madras), the application of the Communal G.O. allocating a specific number of seats for Brahmins would effectively deprive him of admission. Had admissions been determined purely based on marks and without regard to caste or religion, he would have been admitted to the college of his choice.

Champakam Dorairajan was in a similar position. She had secured a BA from Madras University and wanted to enrol into medical college to pursue an MBBS. Her complaint was the same – as a Brahmin, she was put at a disadvantage and would not secure admission because of the Communal G.O. However, there was one fundamental difference between Srinivasan and Dorairajan. Dorairajan did not apply for admission at all – her complaint was made on a speculative basis, following inquiries with the authorities on the prospects of her admission.[8]

The 'full bench' of three judges of the Madras High Court heard arguments in Srinivasan's and Dorairajan's cases (which were clubbed together) from Madras's most prominent lawyers. V.V. Srinivasa Iyengar, described as a 'doyen of the Madras bar',[9] represented Srinivasan. Alladi Krishnaswamy Iyer, former advocate general of Madras and member of the Constituent Assembly, represented Dorairajan. Of Iyer it is said that lawyers 'of the stature of Setalwad and Katju, judges like Patanjali Sastry and N. Rajagopal Iyengar (both of whom were his juniors), politicians, journalists and even famous doctors called on him to savour his wit and wisdom'.[10] Madras was represented by its advocate general, V.K. Thiruvenkatchari.

Iyengar and Iyer argued on behalf of their clients that the Communal G.O. violated two fundamental rights of the newly enacted Constitution. (The fundamental rights are enumerated in Part III of the Constitution.) Article 15(1) prohibited the state from discriminating against any citizen 'on grounds only of religion, race, caste, sex, place of birth or any of them'. Article 29(2) stated that '[n]o citizen shall be denied admission into any educational institution maintained by the state or receiving aid out of state funds on grounds only of religion, race, caste, language or any of them'. Put simply, their argument was that their clients were being denied admission only because of their religion and caste. If admissions were to be determined without reference to those markers of identity, they would have been admitted to the colleges of their choice. The advocate general responded by relying on Article 46, which required the state to 'promote with special care' the educational interests of the 'weaker sections' of the people and protect them from social injustice and exploitation. Article 46 was not a fundamental right, but a directive principle of state policy included in Part IV of the Constitution. The directive principles are an instrument of instructions to the government, which are 'fundamental to the governance of the country'[11] but cannot be enforced on their own terms by the courts.

Each of the three judges of the high court issued a separate opinion. Chief Justice P.V. Rajamannar and Justice Vishwanatha Sastri both agreed that the Communal G.O. should be struck down as unconstitutional to the extent that it sanctioned reservations in college admissions, although they arrived at that decision for different reasons. According to the chief justice, the Communal G.O. prompted an 'obvious disparity' in the treatment of candidates,[12] because a Brahmin candidate with relatively high marks would not secure admission, whereas a non-Brahmin candidate with significantly lower marks would. While the state was obliged to promote the educational interests of weaker sections, that objective could not be achieved by simply any means. The fundamental rights, such as Article 15(1), prescribed limits on the means that the state could deploy to achieve that objective. The chief justice also considered it significant that Articles 15 and 29 of the Constitution did not include a clause analogous to Article 16(4) (which specifically authorized the state to make reservations in government jobs for backward classes of citizens). The logic was that those who drafted the Constitution introduced exceptions to equality where they intended for such exceptions to apply. For the court to hold in the Madras government's favour would be to smuggle in an exception where none existed.

Justice Vishwanatha Sastri held that the Communal G.O. violated Article 15(1) of the Constitution by making caste and religion 'a ground of admission or rejection'.[13] He did not see any merit in the Attorney General's argument based on Article 46 for two reasons. First, the argument was an artificial construct, because the Communal G.O. had existed since well before the Constitution (including Article 46) was enacted. It could hardly be said that the Communal G.O. was made in order to give effect to Article 46. Second, it was unfair to equate the 'weaker sections of society' with non-Brahmin Hindus, an amorphous grouping that had produced 'successive Vice Chancellors of great distinction', 'distinguished Judges', 'competent administrative officers', and 'physicians, surgeons & obstetricians of all-India reputation'.[14]

The third judge of the Madras High Court, Justice N.P. Somasundaram, interpreted the provisions of the Constitution quite differently from his colleagues, though he also hesitantly agreed that the Communal G.O. had to be struck down. He considered the use of the word 'only' in Article 15 significant. Discrimination *solely* on

117

the basis of caste and religion was impermissible, but discrimination on the basis of caste and religion combined with other factors was not. While the government could not discriminate based on caste and religion alone, it could do so if it discriminated, say, based on caste combined with factors such as economic status and levels of education. He also did not lend much weight to the absence of a clause similar to Article 16(4) in Articles 15 and 29. If Article 16(4) simply gave effect to the state's obligation (under Article 46) to promote the educational interests of the 'weaker sections' of the people, the absence of a similar clause in Article 15 did not prevent the state from doing so. In other words, the state's obligation to promote the educational interests of the 'weaker sections' existed independently under Article 46, regardless of whether it was given further effect by a separate clause such as Article 16(4). Probably for the sake of unanimity and in the knowledge that an appeal to the Supreme Court was likely, Justice Somasundaram ultimately agreed with the conclusion that his colleagues arrived at, but 'not without hesitation'.[15] In all but name, Justice Somasundaram's was a dissenting opinion.

Once the Communal G.O. was struck down, discussions were afoot as to what next steps should be taken by the Madras government and the central government. About two weeks after the judgement

118

was handed down by the high court, the law minister of Madras said in the legislative assembly that the government would file an appeal to the Supreme Court. Apart from the legal remedy of filing an appeal, the law minister made it clear that other political remedies were not off the table. This included an amendment to the Constitution to clarify the position and effectively nullify the high court's decision. However, the question of an amendment would only arise, he said, 'after a definite decision had been reached' by the Supreme Court.[16]

The appeal arose for hearing at the Supreme Court in March 1951. At the time, the court had a numerical strength of eight judges including the chief justice. Chief Justice H.J. Kania and six of his colleagues – four of whom would themselves later become chief justice – were on the panel that decided the case. As the hearing progressed, the central government sensed that an adverse decision from the Supreme Court was the most likely outcome. On 17 March, the law ministry sent a note to the cabinet proposing amendments to Article 15 of the Constitution intended to protect measures such as the Communal G.O.[17]

The central government's expectations became a reality. At the end of the hearing, the court indicated to the advocate general that, in a judgement to be delivered in due course, it would be dismissing the appeal and upholding the Madras High Court's decision striking down the Communal G.O.[18] This suggested that the judges were clear about their decision, with little or no disagreement among them. The judgement that followed shortly thereafter was succinct and unanimous, with Justice S.R. Das writing on behalf of the Supreme Court.

The Supreme Court's response to the Madras government's arguments based on Article 46 was that it was a directive principle of state policy that was unenforceable by a court. This principle could not override fundamental rights such as Article 29, because the directive principles 'had to conform to and run as subsidiary to the chapter of fundamental rights'.[19] If the government's argument based on Article 46 was correct, a special provision authorizing reservations, such as Article 16(4), would have been unnecessary to include in the Constitution. The Communal G.O. therefore discriminated on the basis of religion, race and caste and violated the government's obligation under Article 29(2). Since the court arrived at its conclusion on this basis, it decided not to consider the issue of whether the Communal G.O. also violated Article 15.

Four aspects of the Supreme Court's decision were particularly striking. First, the court expressed unease with – but eventually chose to overlook – the fact that one of the litigants, Champakam Dorairajan, did not actually apply for admission.[20] She was effectively representing the group rights of her community (Brahmins) rather than her individual rights.[21] This is arguably among the early antecedents of a disquieting feature of modern public interest litigation in India – where a party that has not itself suffered any injury brings a petition claiming to represent a separate (often amorphous) group of people. Second, Article 29 – which formed the basis of the court's decision – had the title 'protection of the interests of *minorities*'. The court did not engage with the question of how those at the top of the caste hierarchy could claim to be 'minorities'.[22] Third, the logic of the court's interpretation was that reservation was an exception to, rather than a facet of, the right to equality. A meaningful understanding of the right to equality should account for the different conditions and circumstances that people are born into. The court adopted a formal understanding of the right to equality, where (absent specific exceptions) everyone is assumed equal regardless of those conditions and circumstances. This meant that a specific constitutional provision authorizing reservation (such as Article 16[4]) was needed to establish an exception to the right to equality. 'Equality' and 'reservations' became opposites rather than correlatives. Fourth, the court could easily have arrived at the same conclusion without relegating the directive principles to secondary status. The eminent academic Professor P.K. Tripathi described this as 'the most damaging opinion expressed on the value and effectiveness of the directive principles'.[23]

The Supreme Court's decision prompted widespread agitation and protests across the state and in neighbouring areas. The finance minister of Madras travelled to Delhi hoping to persuade Prime Minister Nehru to overturn the decision and restore the Communal G.O. in its entirety. Despite the law ministry note from March, initial news reports indicated that Nehru resisted the pressure and persuasion. One report from May 1951 praised him for declining to amend the Constitution 'to please Madras', with a 'fine disregard for electoral fortunes'.[24] However, that disregard for electoral success did not hold out for long. Within days, an amendment that would effectively nullify the court's decision was included in the bill to make the first amendment to the Constitution, which was being formulated at the time.

There was a menu of options available to the central government in terms of how the Constitution could be amended to nullify the decision. These options included making amendments to Article 15 and Article 29, whether by amending existing clauses within those articles or adding new ones. Among those that advised the government on the form that the constitutional amendment should take was none other than Alladi

Krishnaswamy Iyer, the lawyer who secured a favourable decision for Dorairajan.[25] The formula that was included in the bill added a new clause to Article 15, which provided that neither Article 15 nor Article 29(2) would prevent the state from making special provisions for the 'educational, economic and social' interests of the backward classes.[26]

Since the first general elections were scheduled to take place only in the winter of 1951, this amendment arose for discussion in the provisional Parliament – an 'unusual body'[27] that succeeded (and had broadly the same composition as) the Constituent Assembly. Dr Ambedkar mounted a robust defence of the decision to nullify the Supreme Court's judgement, arguing that the court had misinterpreted the text and scheme of the Constitution. With reference to the text, the court had overlooked the use of the word 'only' in Article 29(2), which ought to have meant that the constitutional prohibition was on deploying caste as the exclusive parameter for discriminating between applicants. No discrimination could be alleged when other parameters, such as economic status and levels of education, were also taken into account. More broadly, the Supreme Court had misread the scheme of the Constitution by making fundamental rights a stumbling block in the advancement of the backward classes.

Through his speech, the former chairperson of the Drafting Committee of the Constitution told the nation that the Supreme Court had got its interpretive analysis of the Constitution completely wrong. On occasion, his criticism of the court turned especially trenchant. His use of the expression 'utterly unsatisfactory' to describe the judgement drew protests from the house and admonishment from the chair. As the atmosphere calmed, Ambedkar produced a witty riposte: 'I have often in the course of my practice told the presiding Judge in very emphatic terms that I am bound to obey his judgement, but I am not bound to respect it. That is the liberty which every lawyer brings in telling the Judge that his judgement is wrong and I am not prepared to give up that liberty.'[28] This speech, lasting over a hundred minutes, was described as 'one of the most outstanding debating performances witnessed in this Parliament' in the *Times of India.*[29]

If Ambedkar presented the legal case, Nehru presented the political case. He rejected the criticism that this amendment adopted a 'communal approach' to the problem, observing that the government's intention was simply to uplift the backward classes. The bill was referred to a select committee of Parliament. The only significant alteration in respect of the amendment that overturned the court's judgement was that the word 'economic' was dropped.[30] That is, the amendment stated that neither Article 15 nor Article 29(2) would prevent the state from making special provisions for the 'educational and social' interests of the backward classes.

The Constitution was amended, and the Dorairajan judgement was overturned efficiently, in a matter of two months. The *Economic and Political Weekly* declared that '[a]t last, after a great deal of controversy, New Delhi saved the Madras Ministry by saving the Communal G.O.'[31]

In some respects, the decision of the Supreme Court in Dorairajan was repudiated in the years that followed. Following that decision, the principle of reservations in educational institutions for scheduled castes, scheduled tribes and socially and educationally backward classes was accepted by the courts.[32] Professor Tripathi would live to see the day when the pendulum swung away from the court's initial position that directive principles were subsidiary to fundamental rights.[33] Directive principles would no longer be seen as running subsidiary to, but would instead be read harmonious with and complement, fundamental rights.

However, in other respects, the court's decision influenced constitutional doctrine long after it was effectively overturned by the provisional Parliament. The idea that reservations are an exception to, rather than a facet of, the right to equality enshrined in the

Constitution persisted. This established and deepened the vocabulary of binaries – such as 'reservations versus merit' – that should never have existed. Seventy years on, Dorairajan continues to cast its long shadow.

7

State of Bombay
v
Narasu Appa Mali

The case that you will now read about is unique among the ten cases discussed in this book. The Supreme Court decides over 50,000 cases a year. Some of these are especially significant from a legal, social or political perspective (and of course, many are not). Almost every important constitutional issue finds its way to the Supreme Court. It is therefore unsurprising that nine out of the ten cases considered in this book were decided by that court, even if they first arose in one of the high courts. This chapter is an exception, for it considers a judgement of the Bombay High Court from 1951 that continues to exert a significant influence on religion and 'personal law' in India. The court's judgement effectively made all uncodified personal law immune from fundamental rights under the Constitution.

~

In contrast with general territorial law (which applies equally to everyone), 'personal law' is the body of law that applies different rules to different religious or ethnic communities. Personal law governs broadly three subject areas – family law (marriage, divorce, custody, alimony and maintenance), aspects of property law (succession, inheritance and wills) and the law governing religious establishments (such as endowments and offices).[1] During colonial rule, general territorial laws were enacted (and interpreted by the courts) as the British Raj consolidated its power. However, the Raj chose to preserve religion-specific personal law rather than replace it with uniform law that applied across communities.

The Regulating Act of 1773 – which named Warren Hastings governor general of Bengal – stated that in all suits concerning marriage, inheritance and caste, the law of the Quran would apply to Muslims and that of the Shastras would apply to Hindus. At this stage, personal law was largely not codified into legislation, but was included in religious texts and scriptures. This personal law was administered through the regular courts. The courts were initially assisted by pandits and kazis, but later administered personal law without any external assistance or advice.[2] These decisions during the early days of the Raj turned out to have 'long-lasting implications'.[3]

During the later years of the Raj, some of the previously uncodified personal law was codified and reformed through legislation. Sati was prohibited by the Bengal Sati Regulation in 1829, and remarriage for Hindu windows permitted by the Hindu Widows' Remarriage Act of 1856. Customary laws that applied to Muslims in various regions prevented Muslim women from inheriting property. The Shariat Act of 1937 substituted the Sharia for these customary laws, paving the way for more robust inheritance rights for Muslim women. The Dissolution of Muslim Marriages Act of 1939 enabled Muslim women to divorce their husbands on a wide range of grounds, including if their husbands failed to perform their 'marital obligations' for three years without reasonable cause. Shortly before Independence, bigamy was prohibited among Hindus in some states, including Baroda and Bombay.

By the final days of the British Raj, personal law was therefore a messy concoction of legislation (codified personal law), uncodified personal law that emanated from religious texts and scriptures, and decisions of courts that interpreted and applied both the codified and the uncodified personal law. The question that arose before the Constituent Assembly of India was whether these complex systems of religion-specific codified and uncodified personal law should remain intact, or whether the Constitution should supplant these separate bodies of law with a 'uniform civil code'. This turned out to be among the most difficult questions for the assembly, for it involved a choice between competing visions of India. Those who supported a uniform civil code argued that it heralded the emergence of a secular, progressive India. Those in favour of retaining personal law appealed to values of inclusiveness and pluralism. The assembly found a compromise solution. Rather than imposing a uniform civil code from the outset, the state was charged with 'endeavour[ing] to secure' a uniform civil code for the country under Article 44.

~

About eighteen months after the Constitution came into force, the Bombay High Court was confronted with an important case involving personal law. Several Hindu men were charged with offences of bigamy under Bombay's bigamy law – the Bombay Prevention of Hindu Bigamous Marriages Act of 1946. This law not only made bigamous marriages invalid among Hindus, but also made it a criminal offence (punishable with up to seven years in prison) for those that entered into such marriages. The cases involving these Hindu men yielded a range of different outcomes. A judge from Mehsana sentenced one of them to six months' rigorous imprisonment and a fine of Rs 100. Another judge from Miraj sentenced two of them to a single day of rigorous imprisonment and a fine of Rs 50. The other two were acquitted, with judges from south Satara and Kaira concluding that the law was unconstitutional. The Bombay High Court was tasked with deciding whether the law was valid, or whether it should be struck down as invalid because it violated the provisions of the Constitution.

This case involved a number of distinguished personalities. The bench consisted of Chief Justice M.C. Chagla and Justice P.B. Gajendragadkar. Chagla is counted among the greatest judges never to have served in the Supreme Court. That was not due to a lack of opportunity – Chagla declined an offer to serve in the Supreme Court because being chief justice of the Bombay High Court (a court of greater antiquity and tradition) was considered far more prestigious at the time.[4] Aside from being a junior in the chambers of Muhammad Ali Jinnah, Chagla was the first Indian chief justice of the Bombay High Court and an ad hoc judge at the International Court of Justice. His judicial career was followed by a distinguished diplomatic career as ambassador to the United States and high commissioner to Britain. Gajendragadkar, who turned fifty in the months before the Narasu case was decided, would be elevated to the Supreme Court five years later and ultimately serve as chief justice of India. C.K. Daphtary, who was solicitor general of India at the time and would later become attorney general, represented the state of Bombay.

The law was challenged on two grounds. First, it was argued that the law violated the right to profess, practise and propagate religion under Article 25 of the Constitution. The court found it relatively easy to reject this argument. Article 25 also permitted the state to provide for 'social welfare and reform'. As Chief Justice Chagla noted, large sections of society considered monogamy 'a very desirable and praiseworthy institution'[5] – a move towards monogamy would therefore constitute social reform. The legislature of the state of Bombay was free to prohibit bigamy in recognition of this. The court was reluctant to displace the view of the legislature on what would, and would not, constitute appropriate social reform.

The other ground on which the law was challenged presented the high court with greater difficulty. The other 'CK' in the case – C.K. Shah, the advocate for the respondents – argued that the law violated the right to equality by applying only to some communities (Hindus, Sikhs, Buddhists, Jains, and followers of the Brahmo Samaj and Arya Samaj) and not others, such as Muslims, Parsis and Christians. Bigamy was, in any event, a criminal offence for Parsis and Christians (but not for Hindus and Muslims) under the IPC.[6] (Bigamy among Hindus was prohibited and became an offence *across* India only with the enactment of the Hindu Marriage Act of 1955.) However, the Bombay bigamy law (which applied only to Hindus) was harsher than the IPC. The offence under the IPC could only be prosecuted upon the complaint of the wife – a requirement that was not imposed by the Bombay law. The Bombay law, unlike the IPC, also did not permit a compromise solution following an agreement with the complainant. The high court saw good reasons for these distinctions. Unlike Parsis and Christians (among whom monogamous relationships were well established), monogamy had been imposed as a measure of social reform among Hindus. The court also noted that it was quite likely that a forbearing Hindu wife would refuse to make a complaint, or in any event would agree to compromise or withdraw that complaint once made. The judges therefore concluded that a more robust law for the Hindus was understandable and justified. This line of reasoning was tenuous in assuming that a Hindu wife was less likely to make a complaint than a Parsi or Christian wife.

Muslims were in a still different position. Bigamy among Muslims was an offence neither under the Bombay law nor under the IPC. This difference in the application of the law prompted, in the words of Chief Justice Chagla, C.K. Shah to make an argument of 'great ingenuity'.[7] Polygamy was permitted by uncodified personal law among Muslim men at the time of Independence and when the Constitution came into force. Apart from the states where it was specifically prohibited before Independence, bigamy was likewise permitted by uncodified personal law among Hindu men at the time. Shah argued that once the Constitution came into force on 26 January 1950, Muslim personal law permitting polygamy as well as Hindu personal law permitting bigamy was inconsistent with fundamental rights under the Constitution and, therefore, invalid. The inconsistency arose from the fact that it discriminated between men and women, by permitting Muslim and Hindu men (but not women) to have more than one spouse. Therefore, according to Shah, even though the Constitution changed the status quo for both Hindu men and Muslim men, the Bombay law only applied to Hindus. In these circumstances, the Bombay law was unconstitutional for singling out and criminalizing bigamy among Hindus and excluding Muslims.

This argument was reliant on the language of Article 13 of the Constitution, which was part of the chapter on fundamental rights. Under Article 13, '[a]ll laws in force in the territory of India' immediately before the commencement of the Constitution would be void to the extent that they were inconsistent with fundamental rights. Did uncodified personal law count as 'law in force' under Article 13? This question assumed particular significance extending beyond the Narasu case. If the court held that personal law was not 'law in force', then all uncodified personal law would effectively be immune from legal challenge on the grounds that it violated fundamental rights.

~

Writing separate decisions, Chief Justice Chagla and Justice Gajendragadkar both held that personal law was not 'law in force' and that the Bombay law was constitutionally valid. They offered a variety of reasons for this decision, some of which were convincing and others less so. Article 13 defined law to include 'custom or usages', leaving the court to decide whether personal law was synonymous with a custom, and therefore should be treated as 'law in force'. The court invoked a constitutional document of colonial India – the Government of India Act of 1915 – in support of its argument that personal law was to be distinguished from custom.

The court cited Section 112 of the Government of India Act of 1915, which laid down the principles for deciding which 'personal law' or 'custom having the force of law' would apply to high court proceedings against the inhabitants of Calcutta, Madras and Bombay. In the court's analysis, the fact that Section 112 used both the phrases 'personal law' and 'custom having the force of law' indicated that they did not have the same meaning. This was a strange argument that equated provisions designed for entirely different purposes. Section 112 determined the law that should be administered by the high courts of Madras, Calcutta and Bombay; Article 13 clarified the effect of an inconsistency between existing laws and the fundamental rights under the Constitution. Unsurprisingly, the debates of the Constituent Assembly do not indicate that Article 13 was modelled on Section 112.

The Bombay High Court also cited Article 17 of the Constitution to reinforce its argument. Article 17 abolished untouchability and its practice in any form. The court held that if personal law was intended to be subject to the scrutiny of fundamental rights, Article 17 would have been superfluous, as all personal law in respect of untouchability would have been invalid because it violated the right to equality. This argument was also unfounded, for at least two reasons. First, Article 17 may well have been included specifically in the Constitution by way of an abundance of caution. In addition, Article 17 was wider than the right to equality, as it applied not just to state actors, but also to private citizens and the public at large. While Article 14 prohibited 'the state' from denying equality before the law, Article 17 made no analogous reference to the state or public officials.

The court's next justification invoked Article 372 of the Constitution, which permitted the President within the first three years to make adaptations or modifications to any 'law in force' – the same phrase used in Article 13 – to bring it into conformity with the Constitution. The high court observed that the Constituent Assembly cannot have intended to permit the President to unilaterally modify personal law. Therefore, the court concluded that 'law in force' did not include personal law, whether under Article 13 or Article 372. In arriving at this conclusion, the court assumed that the same words used in entirely different chapters of the Constitution should be ascribed the same meaning. Article 13 is included in the chapter on fundamental rights, while Article 372 is included in a chapter entitled 'temporary, transitional and special provisions'. Ultimately, as one prominent scholar described it, what the court was doing was to treat personal law as 'off-limits'.[8]

Once the Bombay High Court decided that the bigamy law was constitutionally valid, it turned to the punishments imposed on the defendants. In possible recognition of the draconian effect of the law, the court reduced the terms of imprisonment in almost every case. A sentence of imprisonment was replaced with a fine of Rs 100 for one defendant whose second marriage took place with the 'consent and approval' of his first wife. Sentences of imprisonment were considered harsh for three other defendants, and were reduced to fines of Rs 50 or less. For yet another defendant, the court reduced the sentence to the term of imprisonment already served by the defendant, and imposed a fine of Rs 25.

Two important factors played a role in the high court's decision-making process. First, the court was sensitive about the task of interpreting or commenting on religious practices. Chief Justice Chagla, himself a Muslim, expressed 'very considerable hesitation' to speak 'about the Hindu religion'.[9] Second, the court was also conscious of the compromise that the Constituent Assembly arrived at in the form of Article 44. For Justice

Gajendragadkar, the assembly's impatience in seeking a uniform civil code was only 'tempered by considerations of practical difficulties'.[10] For Chief Justice Chagla, Article 44 laid down a directive that would have been expected to be achieved 'within a measurable time'.[11] Although the judges were conscious of the significance of their decision – effectively insulating uncodified personal law from the scrutiny of fundamental rights – they did so in the belief that it would remain relevant only for a brief period.

~

The Narasu judgement offered up a mixture of contradictions. On the one hand, the high court upheld the Bombay Prevention of Hindu Bigamous Marriages Act, a seemingly liberal, progressive law that was directed towards eradicating and punishing a social evil. The court was clearly 'motivated by public concern'.[12] However, the court's chosen method of arriving at that destination – by holding that all personal law was protected from rights-based challenges – had the potential to safeguard regressive religious practices indefinitely.

Was the court driven to a binary choice by the 'ingenuity' of C.K. Shah's argument – uphold progressive legislation and risk safeguarding regressive religious practice, or strike down progressive legislation and leave open the possibility of challenging regressive religious practice in the future? The court could have escaped this binary by arriving at the same decision in respect of Muslims as it did for Parsis and Christians – that even though polygamy is no longer recognized under Muslim personal law, there were good reasons for making it a criminal offence among Hindus but not Muslims. This was a missed opportunity.

The Bombay High Court's judgement also generated a different kind of paradox. Uncodified personal law that carried over from colonial rule would occupy a higher position than law enacted by democratically elected legislatures. While ordinary law covering any subject (including religion) could be challenged on the basis that it violated fundamental rights, uncodified personal law was now effectively free from scrutiny in the courts. Conversely, if and when personal law was codified by the democratically elected legislature, that would be subjected to greater judicial scrutiny than uncodified personal law lacking democratic sanction.

Not surprisingly, then, many progressive, pro-women decisions of various courts have been in respect of enacted law rather than uncodified personal law. Most prominent (and controversial) among these was the Shah Bano case,[13] which addressed the question of whether a Muslim divorcee would be entitled to a maintenance allowance from her ex-husband under Section 125 of the Criminal Procedure Code (CrPC). The ex-husband, Mohammed Ahmed Khan, argued that his payment of a small sum under religious personal law ('mahr') exempted him from any further obligation to make payments. The Supreme Court rejected this argument, deciding that Khan would pay a monthly sum of maintenance to his ex-wife.

The judgement courted tremendous controversy, with the Rajiv Gandhi government ultimately deciding in favour of overturning it through legislation. However, soon after the law was enacted, several high courts (and later, the Supreme Court) effectively restored the position that Muslim women had a right to maintenance after divorce.[14] This was done through a 'gender-sensitive interpretation'[15] of the legislation enacted by the Rajiv Gandhi government, with the courts holding that the new legislation replaced the right to claim periodic maintenance payments under the CrPC with a right to claim a one-time divorce settlement. There are many other examples of the courts making liberal decisions in the context of enacted law. In one case, the Supreme Court held that a law enacted during the British Raj preventing Christians from bequeathing property for religious and charitable purposes was unconstitutional.[16]

At the turn of the century, several high courts struck down a law that afforded Christian women narrower grounds for divorce than men.

However, the story was different in respect of personal law that remained uncodified. As a senior lawyer put it, the 'ghost' of Narasu has continued to haunt courts across the country.[17] In one case in 1979, the question addressed to the courts was whether a Dalit was legally permitted to become a sanyasi. In a judgement that cut against the rationale in the Narasu case, the Allahabad High Court held that the personal law preventing Dalits from becoming sanyasis violated fundamental rights and became unconstitutional once the Constitution was enacted. However, the Supreme Court decisively reverted to Narasu, holding that fundamental rights do not have any bearing on personal law. Judges could not, in the court's words, infuse personal law with 'concepts of modern times' but were duty-bound to enforce the law as contained in religious scriptures and commentaries.[18]

Narasu was upheld once again by the Supreme Court in 1997.[19] An NGO filed a Public Interest Litigation (PIL) challenging several aspects of Hindu and Muslim law on the basis that they violated fundamental rights. The NGO's wish list to the court included a declaration that Muslim personal law permitting polygamy was unconstitutional and a declaration that Sunni and Shia law in respect of inheritance discriminated against women. The Supreme Court refused to delve into these issues in any detail, noting that these were matters best left to the political process. In its short judgement, it extensively cited Narasu and the proposition that personal law was immune from fundamental rights challenges. The court's decision was somewhat ironic, for in leaving these matters to Parliament in the spirit of democracy, it upheld a judgement that elevated uncodified personal law above democratically enacted law.

In 2018, the court was presented with another opportunity of setting right the mistakes of Narasu, or at the least acknowledging that the atmosphere in which that decision was made (an imminent uniform civil code) had long ceased to exist. Muslim women approached the court claiming that the practice of 'instant triple talaq' was unconstitutional. It was widely anticipated that the bench of five judges allocated to hear the case would bury Narasu once and for all. The majority of judges struck down the practice of instant triple talaq, but they did so on different grounds – namely, that instant triple talaq was not integral to Islamic practice and was therefore not part of personal law at all.[20] The most robust statement about Narasu that would come from the bench was simply that 'it may be necessary to have a re-look' at this decision in a 'suitable case'.[21]

There have been some notable exceptions from this trend. In a decision upholding women's right to worship at the Sabarimala temple in Kerala, one judge of the Supreme Court noted that Narasu was incorrectly decided and detracted 'from the notion that no body of practices can claim supremacy over the Constitution and its vision of ensuring the sanctity of dignity, liberty and equality'.[22] In 1996, a judge of the Supreme Court observed that personal laws imposing an inferior status on women were 'anathema to equality' and must be consistent with the Constitution, including fundamental rights.[23] Another powerful criticism of the Narasu judgement came from the Kerala High Court: '[w]ith great respect to the eminent Judges who decided [the case] ... we feel that the decision requires reconsideration.'[24] The high court also observed that there was no reason to insulate personal law from scrutiny in a secular republic, and to do so went against India's 'core constitutional values'.[25] These voices have been unable to persuade the Supreme Court to decisively overturn Narasu.

~

Close to seven decades after the Bombay High Court's decision in Narasu, the judgement remains good law. This means that in the world's largest constitutional

144

democracy, one category of law (uncodified personal law) is effectively above the Constitution itself. To be sure, the courts have often found ways of sidestepping the decision – by holding that a practice claimed to be personal law is not personal law at all, or that a practice within personal law has in fact been codified by statute. 'Minimalism' in decision-making has also played its part, with the courts sometimes ruling that they did not strictly need to consider whether Narasu was correctly decided in order to arrive at a decision on the facts before them. Yet, the ultimate overruling of Narasu would be of some substantive, and tremendous symbolic, significance. It would take us some distance in the quest to establishing that the true meaning of constitutional supremacy is that the Constitution is above all other law, regardless of its source or origin. In theory, Parliament can also overturn Narasu with a simple amendment to Article 13 of the Constitution, but there seems to be little political appetite to do so.

Every judgement must be read in its own time and context. Narasu was decided soon after the Constitution was enacted. The two towering personalities that decided the case conceived of Narasu as a transitional judgement that would become moot once a uniform civil code was enacted. Regardless of that socio-political context and purely as a matter of legal interpretation, the Bombay

High Court was wrong to decide as it did. Even the most distinguished judges are prone to error. The greater error lies in the failure to make course corrections despite ample opportunity.

Part 4

National Security

8

Kartar Singh

v

State of Punjab

Threats to national security, whether real or imagined, are often a trump card for governments around the world. 'National security' is a shield that protects legitimate government action, but it can often be a cover for a multitude of sins. When governments defend their conduct citing national security concerns, courts tend to freeze. In England, the House of Lords caved in when confronted with a set of sweeping preventive detention regulations during the Second World War. In a celebrated dissenting opinion, Lord Atkin described the decision of the majority as 'more executive minded than the executive'.[1] Just three months later, President

Franklin Roosevelt signed an order requiring Japanese Americans to relocate to internment camps in the name of national security and protection against espionage. When Roosevelt's order was challenged, the US Supreme Court abdicated its responsibility to uphold fundamental rights. Justice Robert H. Jackson dissented that day, lamenting that 'the Court for all time has validated the principle of racial discrimination'.[2]

India's corresponding moment was the ADM Jabalpur case of 1976,[3] where the Supreme Court denied citizens' most cherished fundamental rights in response to executive demands for deference during Indira Gandhi's contrived Emergency of 1975. The court held that those who had been detained under preventive detention legislation were effectively barred from challenging their detention in the courts, since the right to life and other fundamental rights had been suspended. Justice H.R. Khanna wrote a powerful dissent that cost him the position of chief justice of India – he was due to be elevated to the position in 1977 but instead a judge junior to him, Justice M.H. Beg, whose decision in the same case was sympathetic to the government, was elevated to the position. ADM Jabalpur is a judgement that India *will not* forget. However, this chapter considers a judgement that India *should not* forget. The Kartar Singh case[4] included similar features – the government played the 'national security' card, the court deferred to the government's position in the knowledge that doing so would violate fundamental rights, and citizens were left without a remedy. Only, in this case there was no significant voice of conscience from within the court such as Justice Jackson, Lord Atkin or Justice Khanna.

~

The Terrorists and Disruptive Activities Act – better known as TADA – was enacted in 1985 in the backdrop of militant groups engaging in guerrilla-style conflict in Punjab, Kashmir, Andhra Pradesh and parts of the Northeast. However, the immediate catalyst for TADA was the assassination of Indira Gandhi by her Sikh bodyguards in October 1984. The parliamentary debates leading up to the enactment of TADA were high on histrionics. One Congress MP observed, 'In the rivers of Punjab milk used to flow but they are now drenched with blood. There is hatred all over.' Another warned the house that terrorism was not a problem restricted to Punjab – it had 'spread to every corner of the country'. And yet another cautioned, as if to sum up the situation: 'We are not dealing with normal peaceful times. We are dealing with extraordinary times.'

Initially enacted as a temporary measure for a period of two years, TADA was re-enacted in 1987 – once again for a two-year period. TADA originally applied only to Punjab and its neighbouring states. Thereafter, it was periodically extended both in time (from two years to four, four to six, and six to eight) and in its geographical breadth of application. By the mid-1990s, TADA had been in force for nearly a decade and applied to twenty-three states and two union territories. More than ninety-five per cent of the citizens now came within its purview.[5]

TADA set up, in effect, a parallel criminal justice process and special courts for the speedy trial of those accused of terrorism. Some of its provisions were especially draconian. Under criminal law, it was the prosecution's burden to prove its case against the defendant. TADA reversed the burden of proof on to defendants in certain cases. With a view to safeguarding against custodial torture, the rules of evidence did not allow confessions procured in police custody to be admitted as evidence. TADA altered existing procedural safeguards by making confessions to senior police officers admissible. Defendants anticipating arrest could ordinarily apply for 'anticipatory bail' (a direction for release of the person on bail even before they are arrested). TADA not only negated the right to apply for anticipatory bail, but also made it more difficult to secure bail *after arrest*. Criminal appeals would normally proceed from the subordinate criminal courts to the state high court, with a further appeal to the Supreme Court. TADA eliminated one layer of appeal, by denying rights of appeal to state high courts and providing for direct appeal to the Supreme Court.

In the years after it was enacted, TADA became an instrument of oppression in the hands of the police and state authorities. A disproportionate number of those charged with offences under TADA were Muslims and Sikhs.[6] TADA was also frequently invoked in states that lacked a consistent history of terrorist violence, including Gujarat and Maharashtra. Despite the odds being stacked against the accused, conviction rates were embarrassingly low, with estimates ranging from 1 per cent to 4 per cent. This implied that only a small minority of those detained under TADA were ever proven, on evidence, to be terrorists. Especially because of its strict provisions on bail, under TADA the process was the punishment. Those that were ultimately acquitted had often spent many years in prison, sacrificing their family lives, reputations and careers.

Newspaper reports were replete with examples of frivolous or inappropriate cases filed under TADA. In one case, two men were charged under TADA for creating a ruckus at Byculla market in Bombay by wielding a gun, which turned out to be a toy gun. They were detained for two years before they could secure bail.[7] In another instance, three boys were arrested for possessing 'sutli' bombs – commonly used as firecrackers – and spent four years in prison.[8] A series of cases where TADA was applied to gangsters or ordinary criminals (including a garment exporter suspected of tax evasion) in Maharashtra compelled the additional public prosecutor, in 1991, to concede that TADA was being misapplied.[9]

Since TADA made it harder to secure bail than the ordinary criminal law, it also became a trend for the police to bring TADA charges to keep a defendant in prison when he secured bail. The Maharashtra Police, for instance, charged a man accused of threatening and chasing a driver with a knife under TADA after they were incensed by the success of his bail application.[10] The Punjab director general of police, in 1987, virtually admitted that TADA was used as a tool for preventive detention.[11] As one scholar put it, TADA 'enabled pervasive use of preventive detention and a variety of abuses by the police, including extortion and torture'.[12]

Together with the frivolous and inappropriate, there were also the politically motivated. A journalist was arrested for writing about militants attaching posters to village walls in Assam. In another case, the leader of a Muslim women's organization was incarcerated with her one-year-old son.[13] Those with access to the corridors of power managed to escape more quickly. Shabnam Lone, the daughter of Abdul Ghani Lone (the founder of the

People's Conference in Kashmir) and a junior in the chambers of prominent senior advocate K.K. Venugopal, was arrested under TADA. She secured bail within hours by filing a petition directly in the Supreme Court.[14] The unconnected weren't quite so lucky.

Soon after TADA was implemented, petitions challenging its validity on constitutional grounds began to be filed in the Supreme Court. The number of petitions challenging TADA increased over time, some reports suggesting that over a thousand petitions had been filed by 1991.[15] Even as tens of thousands of people were charged under TADA, these petitions gathered dust in the Supreme Court's roster. In an interview a full seven years after the first petitions were filed, R.S. Sodhi (a leading criminal lawyer who represented several TADA defendants in the Supreme Court) lamented the delay and said that he did not expect the court to decide the petitions any time soon.[16]

When the case ultimately arose for hearing in early 1994, a 'galaxy of senior lawyers',[17] including Ram Jethmalani, K.T.S. Tulsi and V.M. Tarkunde, appeared on both sides. Over sixty lawyers in total recorded appearance. TADA was subjected to two distinct lines of attack in the Supreme Court: first, that Parliament lacked the legislative authority to enact the law, and second, that many of its provisions violated fundamental rights under the Constitution. Although these were analytically separate grounds of challenge, as it turned out, success on the first ground of challenge had a significant impact on the prospects of success for the second ground.

Judgement was delivered on a spring day in March 1994. On the eve of his retirement, Justice S.R. Pandian delivered the leading opinion on behalf of three of the five judges. The other two judges – Justices K. Ramaswamy and R.M. Sahai – wrote separate opinions disagreeing with some aspects of the majority decision. The Constitution distributes legislative powers (to Parliament on the one hand and the state legislatures on the other) through three lists. Parliament has exclusive power to make laws on matters within the Union List, the state legislatures have exclusive power to make laws on matters within the State List, while both have the power to make laws on matters within the Concurrent List. On the first ground of challenge, the question before the court was whether TADA addressed the 'defence of India' (which formed part of the Union List) and was therefore within the authority of Parliament, as the central government argued, or whether it was directed towards 'public order' (which formed part of the State List) and was therefore unconstitutional as it was within the legislative authority of the states.

Confronted with doomsday scenarios of terrorism of the 1980s ('bloodbath, firing, looting and killing, [converting parts of the country into] a graveyard'),[18] Justice Pandian held unambiguously in favour of the government on the first ground of challenge. To ignore that thousands of innocents were losing their lives to terrorism would be to adopt 'an ostrich like attitude completely ignoring the impending danger'.[19] TADA was directed towards addressing activities that threatened the security and integrity of the country as a whole rather than public order in any particular state. Therefore, it was within Parliament's legislative authority to enact TADA, the court said.

The second basis of challenge was more contentious. Those challenging TADA argued that many of its provisions were especially draconian and diminished safeguards available under the general criminal law. For example, as mentioned earlier, confessions made to police officers (which are otherwise not admissible as evidence) were made admissible in TADA cases, so long as those confessions were made to officers of sufficient seniority. The rule against admission of confessional evidence procured in police custody was an essential safeguard in the context of the long history of custodial torture in India. Even if the rule did not deter custodial torture and forced confessions, at least it did not further incentivize them. The petitioners therefore argued that Section 15 of TADA, which departed from this safeguard, violated the fundamental right to equality (by denying a safeguard to terrorist suspects that others were entitled to under the law) and life (by incentivizing custodial torture).

Justice Pandian's decision on this question was a judgement of two halves. In the first, he powerfully condemned custodial torture and the practice of securing confessions by coercion. Drawing upon their experiences as lawyers and judges, he and his colleagues lamented that they 'frequently dealt with cases of atrocity and brutality practiced by some overzealous police officers' who resorted to 'inhuman, barbaric, archaic and drastic' measures.[20] The court knew only too well that these measures were taken with the view of collecting evidence 'by hook or by crook'.[21] The decision condemned these 'degrading and despicable'[22] practices adopted by some police officers.

These observations should have made the conclusion inevitable. The court ought to have struck down Section 15 on the grounds that it denied the most basic safeguards against custodial torture and violated the right to life. There was substantial support to arrive at this conclusion in existing principles laid down by the Supreme Court. The second half of Justice Pandian's decision, however, did not logically follow from the first. Despite the judges' serious misgivings about Section 15 'at the first impression',[23] the court ultimately decided not to strike it down.

Among the reasons offered by the court for eventually upholding Section 15 were that Parliament was within its authority to enact that section, that terrorism was endangering the integrity of the nation, and that victims and the public were reluctant to come forward to give evidence in the absence of a robust anti-terrorism law. More fundamentally, however, the court appeared to surrender in the face of the 'emergency, problem-solving'[24] legislation that TADA was.[25] To strike down one of the key elements of TADA in a time of crisis was perhaps a step too far. One of the judges (Justice Ramaswamy) dissented, but himself refused to strike down Section 15 with immediate effect – preferring to suspend it for a year to enable Parliament to make amendments to the law.

The court then issued a series of anodyne guidelines in an attempt to regulate the misuse of Section 15. These guidelines included that confessions be recorded in the same language in which the person was examined, that defendants who made confessions be produced before a magistrate without any delay, that the police be required to respect the defendants' right to silence, and that a committee be set up at the central and state levels to review the functioning of TADA.

The court approached other sections of TADA that were challenged in a similar way. Section 19, for example, denied defendants the right to appeal to the state high court, instead providing for a direct appeal from special courts established under TADA to the Supreme Court. By leapfrogging the high court, Section 19 not only deprived defendants of one avenue of appeal, but also had financial implications for those defendants based away from Delhi. This principle would apply even in cases where a defendant who was charged for committing offences under TADA and other criminal legislation was acquitted for the TADA offences but convicted for offences under the ordinary criminal law. The central government held out Section 19 as a crucial part of its strategy in securing swift trials in anti-terrorism cases.

Again, at first, Justice Pandian's opinion identified the serious problems with Section 19. Defendants from remote parts of the country with limited access to resources would effectively be denied a right of appeal as litigation in the Supreme Court is far more financially onerous than in a high court. To deny an appeal to the high court when defendants were merely charged (but not convicted) under TADA seemed illogical. Section 19, according to Justice Pandian, was an 'abnormal procedure' that 'denied fair play and justice'.[26] This unequivocal criticism did not result in a strikedown of Section 19.

Instead, Section 19 was merely described as posing 'practical difficulties'[27] and upheld.

Section upon section of TADA – addressing matters such as the creation of special courts and the denial of 'anticipatory bail' for TADA offences – was upheld by the Supreme Court. The court struck down only a single section of TADA, which permitted identification through photographs rather than identification parades. This was somewhat peculiar, since neither of the parties addressed this issue in their submissions to the court.

The public reaction to the Supreme Court's decision was mixed. Some news reports in the immediate aftermath indicated that the decision would curb the misuse of TADA. A story in the *Times of India* carried the title 'SC ruling blunts TADA stringency'. The court had blunted the 'oppressive portions' of TADA despite upholding it, it said.[28] Scholarly opinion, however, was far less generous. One incisive commentary published in the *Economic and Political Weekly* described it as a judgement that was 'poor in language', 'poor in judicial philosophy' and 'poor in logic', that 'ruthlessly' put defendants in terrorism cases beyond the realm of the Constitution.[29]

To those familiar with the trajectory of the Supreme Court's constitutional decisions, the Kartar Singh judgement was seen as an outright abandonment of recent precedent that demanded a more rigorous analysis of legislation enacted by Parliament. Fundamental rights were meant to be robust guarantees against legislative action, with judicial deference to Parliament being a thing of the past. At best, the court's decision disregarded the real problems caused by the parallel criminal justice process that TADA established. At worst, the court's decision placed a stamp of endorsement on the 'most tyrannical of laws'[30] – one that in practice imposed heavy burdens upon those who could least withstand them. The court demonstrated that it was still capable of being – to borrow Lord Atkin's words once again – 'more executive minded than the executive'.

Only a few months before the Kartar Singh judgement, a new human rights body – the National Human Rights Commission (NHRC) – was set up by the Narasimha Rao-led Congress government. The NHRC was set up in response to fears of an international backlash following widespread reports of custodial violence and police atrocities. Ranganath Misra, former chief justice of India, was the first chairperson of the NHRC.

The NHRC was openly dissatisfied with the Supreme Court's decision in the Kartar Singh case. In 1994, it adopted a 'three-pronged strategy' to address the problems that TADA gave rise to. First, it monitored the implementation of TADA by the police and public officials on the ground. Second, it prepared a dossier seeking to convince the Supreme Court to reconsider its decision. Third, it worked towards convincing MPs not to renew TADA as its renewal date (in 1995) drew close yet again. The third strategy was the most significant, as developing a public consensus against renewing TADA was preferable to the uncertainty of litigation.

Justice Misra was personally invested in ensuring that TADA was not renewed. In a letter to MPs, he strongly condemned the law and observed that the NHRC would not be in a position to fulfil its mandate if the statute remained on the books. Justice Misra also gave several interviews and delivered lectures advocating that TADA not be renewed. In Hyderabad, he commented on the large number of TADA cases that had been filed in Andhra Pradesh, despite it being relatively peaceful.[31] The position he took in interviews was decisive: 'The opportunity to have a fair trial . . . is totally taken away . . . The law was wrong from the inception. How is it that a free country can have a law like this today?'[32]

These efforts proved successful as sufficient political support was galvanized to ensure that TADA would not be renewed beyond 23 May 1995. This was a major early accomplishment for the NHRC. Ten years and tens of thousands of cases later, TADA was finally no longer in force. Nevertheless, TADA continued to live an afterlife following its expiry, as existing prosecutions under TADA were preserved and continued unabated many years after it was off the books. India forgot TADA – but some Indians did not.

9

Naga People's Movement of
Human Rights
v
Union of India

The judgement that is the subject matter of this chapter offers yet another example of the Supreme Court abdicating its responsibility to protect fundamental rights when the government plays the 'national security' card. Even as in the 1990s the court was breaking new ground and interpreting the Constitution expansively in other cases, it toed the line and accepted the establishment narrative in this case. Following a fifteen-year wait for the case involving the constitutionality of the Armed Forces Special Powers Act (AFSPA) to be decided, inhabitants of the Northeast discovered that the more things changed, the more they remained the same.

~

The AFSPA was enacted in 1958 in response to insurgency and demands for self-determination in the Northeast. Initially, Prime Minister Jawaharlal Nehru's reaction to the Naga rebellion was to send in the army with instructions to act with caution. The army was ordered to treat the rebels as 'fellow Indians' and to use proportionate force. However, the AFSPA came into being as the rebellion intensified. G.B. Pant, the home minister at the time, justified the law stating that it was necessary to enable the armed forces to address the rebellion effectively. But the law was not passed unopposed. In a particularly prescient criticism, an MP from Inner Manipur described it as an 'anti-democratic measure' and a 'lawless law'.[1] Another MP described it as a 'legal monstrosity'.[2] Despite these pockets of trenchant criticism, the AFSPA was enacted unamended following seven hours of debate in both houses of Parliament.

The AFSPA was not drafted on a clean slate – its ancestry can be traced back to a series of laws enacted in the 1940s.[3] One of them – the Armed Forces (Special Powers) Ordinance of 1942 – was promulgated by the

British viceroy of India, Lord Linlithgow, one week into the Quit India movement. The rationale offered for the 1942 Ordinance was that it was in response to the 'emergency' that had arisen which made it 'necessary to confer certain special powers upon certain officers of the armed forces'. This colonial lineage may have been ironic, but was not surprising. As a member of the Indian Civil Service put it, there was a 'tradition of decision-making by precedent inherent in the administrative processes and inherited from the predecessor government' and it was oddly assumed that 'the British technique of dealing with a situation was necessarily the correct technique'.[4] Another predecessor to the AFSPA of 1948 was enacted by the Constituent Assembly shortly after Independence. On that occasion, Pandit Thakur Das Bhargava cautioned the assembly against enacting this 'very drastic' law that undermined the rights of the people.[5]

As enacted in 1958, the AFSPA was a brief piece of legislation. It had only seven sections – but those sections comprised the difference between accountability and impunity. It enabled the governor of the state (and later, also the central government) to declare any part of any state (or indeed, the whole of the state) to which it applied as a 'disturbed area'. The AFSPA initially applied to Assam and Manipur, but was extended to all seven north-eastern states following the reorganization of states in that region.

The real sting of the AFSPA was in Section 4. It conferred certain special powers – or as some might say, near-unlimited powers – on members of the armed forces operating in 'disturbed areas'. These special powers assumed four manifestations, which can colloquially be described as the licences to kill, destroy, arrest and search. The 'licence to kill'[6] was the most draconian of these provisions. It permitted a member of the armed forces to fire upon or kill any person who violated a law or an order: (a) that prohibited the assembly of five or more people, or (b) that prohibited carrying weapons or explosives. The threshold to invoke this licence was especially low and vague. The member of the armed forces only needed to be of the subjective opinion that the use of force was necessary to maintain public order. The AFSPA did not require members of the armed forces to provide a warning before exercising lethal force – they were offered the option of giving any warning they considered necessary.

The 'licence to destroy' permitted the destruction of not only any arms dump, but also any structure used as a training camp, or simply a hideout, by armed gangs. Then there was the 'licence to arrest' any person suspected of having committed a cognizable offence (serious offences for which, under ordinary law, the police can make arrests without a warrant from a magistrate). Finally, the 'licence to search' enabled searches of any premises to make arrests or recover stolen property or ammunition. The AFSPA required that any person who was arrested by the armed forces be handed over to the police 'with the least possible delay'.[7] Finally, no legal proceedings could be initiated against any member of the armed forces acting under the AFSPA without the prior permission of the central government. Simply put, no permission would mean no prosecution, regardless of how serious the allegations were.

After the AFSPA was enacted, large parts of Assam and Manipur were designated as 'disturbed areas'. This was eventually extended to the whole of Assam and Manipur, as well as parts of Nagaland, Mizoram, Tripura, Arunachal Pradesh and Meghalaya. The AFSPA acquired notoriety early into its operation. Rather than aiding the civil administration in disturbed areas, the army effectively operated a parallel administration in those areas. Counter-insurgency methods against the Nagas and Mizos included 'village regrouping', or the 'forced relocation of civilians in camps under close surveillance'.[8] For instance, in the late 1960s, over 1,30,000 Mizos were regrouped into just over a hundred regrouping centres guarded by the army.[9] Torture, rape, arbitrary detention and killing inflicted by those in uniform became increasingly common occurrences.

By the early 1980s, petitions began to be filed in the Supreme Court and the Gauhati High Court (which at the time was the only high court for the seven states in the Northeast). Some of these petitions challenged the decisions of the government to notify areas as 'disturbed', while others challenged the constitutional validity of the AFSPA itself. Among the petitioners in the high court was Indrajit Barua, a civil engineer and alumnus of the Indian Institute of Technology Kharagpur.[10]

When Barua's petition arose for hearing at the Gauhati High Court in 1980, Justice B.L. Hansaria made the courageous decision of ordering a stay on the enforcement of Section 4(a) of the AFSPA, the 'licence to kill' section. This set the cat among the pigeons. The Congress government at the centre, together with the Assam state government, approached the Supreme Court asking that Barua's petition (together with a group of similar petitions) be transferred out of Gauhati. They argued that agitations and protests were taking place across the state, that the Assam Judicial Officers' Association had resolved to support the agitations, and therefore the atmosphere in the state was not conducive to a fair trial.[11] Tactically, the central and state governments would have conceived of their prospects of success as far more favourable in the distant Delhi High Court than in a court that was nearer the epicentre of the insurgency.

The petition filed by the central and state governments was first heard out of term, that is, when the Supreme Court was in recess. Justice Kailasam, the 'vacation judge' (the judge of the Supreme Court who is tasked with hearing cases while the court is in recess), stayed proceedings in the Gauhati High Court until the Supreme Court could decide the case during term time.[12] Upon hearing the case during term time, the Supreme Court agreed to transfer the petitions from the Gauhati High Court to the Delhi High Court. The Supreme Court arrived at this decision despite the arguments of leading senior advocate Dr Y.S. Chitale that a tense atmosphere may have an impact on the investigation – but not the adjudication – of a case.[13] The court also emphasized the administrative convenience for the government of the petitions being heard in Delhi as opposed to Gauhati. This logic was criticized by scholars as it implied that every case involving the central government should be heard in Delhi rather than at the relevant state high court.

The central government's strategy of seeking a transfer of the petitions to the Delhi High Court yielded dividends. On 3 June 1983, a bench of two judges of the Delhi High Court rejected the challenges to the constitutional validity of the AFSPA. The court accepted that collective security would trump individual rights and liberties: 'Social imperatives for the greater good

171

must take precedence,'[14] the court said. The court was also convinced by the argument that the AFSPA was in operation in a sensitive geographic region, with 'China and Nepal in the North and North West, Burma in the East and Bangladesh (formerly E. Pakistan) in the South'.[15]

While this strategic game of petitions and transfers was playing out in the high courts, separate petitions challenging the constitutional validity of the AFSPA were being filed in the Supreme Court. These petitions began piling up, with petitioners which included prominent human rights organizations such as the People's Union for Democratic Rights, the Naga People's Movement for Human Rights and the Human Rights Forum. The petitions gathered dust for over one and a half decades, with no hearings taking place and the constitutional challenge remaining undecided. In that time, India had witnessed seven new prime ministers – from Rajiv Gandhi to I.K. Gujral – being sworn into office. No less than eleven chief justices of the Supreme Court (from Justice Y.V. Chandrachud to Justice A.M. Ahmadi) had retired from office during that period. Laws almost identical to the AFSPA were enacted and applied first to Punjab[16] (in 1983) and later to Jammu and Kashmir (in 1990).[17]

As the petitions remained pending, the human cost of the AFSPA was incalculable. Over a dozen women were gang-raped by paramilitary forces in a period of three days in 1988 in the village of Ujanmaidan in Tripura. In 1995, soldiers began shooting indiscriminately in Kohima after mistaking the sound of a tyre bursting for a bomb blast. Seven people (including two children) were killed, and twenty-two were injured as a result.[18] In a separate incident the same year, a man was arrested on suspicion of being an insurgent in Purana Bazar, Nagaland. Two days after his arrest, he died in the custody of paramilitary forces under suspicious circumstances.[19]

Eventually, it was the twelfth chief justice since the petitions were filed – Justice J.S. Verma – who constituted a five-judge bench of the Supreme Court to hear these petitions in a consolidated proceeding in 1997. (It bears repetition that these petitions had been in the judicial queue since the early 1980s!) Apart from Justice Verma himself, the bench consisted of Justice S.C. Agrawal and three other judges who would themselves become chief justices – Justices M.M. Punchhi, A.S. Anand and S.P. Bharucha. Several prominent advocates appeared on all sides. Attorney General Ashok Desai represented the central government. The NHRC was permitted to intervene, with Rajeev Dhavan appearing on its behalf. Those that appeared on behalf of the petitioners included Shanti Bhushan, Indira Jaising and Kapil Sibal.

The challenge to the AFSPA was two-pronged. The

first was that Parliament lacked the legislative authority to enact the law, as it addressed subject matter – public order – that was within the domain of the state legislatures. The second was that the provisions of the AFSPA nevertheless violated fundamental rights under the Constitution, and should be struck down on that basis. After the delay of over fifteen years, the court mercifully took only three months following the conclusion of the hearing to pronounce judgement in the winter of 1997. For the multitude of NGOs and human rights organizations that opposed the AFSPA, the judgement was not worth the wait.

A large bench increases the odds of multiple opinions and disagreements among the judges. In this instance, however, there was unanimity expressed in a single voice. The opinion was written by Justice Agrawal and signed by Chief Justice Verma and the three other chief justices in waiting. The Supreme Court rejected the argument that the AFSPA addressed 'public order', a subject that was within the domain of the state legislatures rather than Parliament. In 1976, the 'public order' entry in the State List had been amended to specifically carve out a power for Parliament to deploy the army, navy or air force 'in aid of civil power'. Relying on this amendment, the court noted that the AFSPA concerned 'the use of armed forces in aid of the civil power' (which was within Parliament's authority) and not 'public order' (which was within the authority of the state legislatures). The court also relied on Article 355 of the Constitution, which imposes a duty on the union to protect every state from internal disturbance, in arriving at this conclusion.

The petitioners also presented an alternative, innovative argument challenging Parliament's authority to enact the AFSPA. This argument was that the AFSPA would enable the government to circumvent the emergency provisions of the Constitution. A declaration that an area was disturbed under the AFSPA resembled an undeclared emergency, but did not enlist the constitutional safeguards and processes that would come into play if an emergency was formally declared. The court did not address this argument head-on, simply reaffirming that it was within the competence of Parliament (rather than the state legislatures) to enact the AFSPA. These were two analytically separate arguments, but the court wrongly treated them as one and the same.[20]

As it turned out, after the court spent much of its time addressing the argument that the AFSPA was beyond Parliament's legislative authority, it had little appetite to address the second argument. Section after section of the AFSPA was upheld by the court on the grounds that it was not arbitrary or unreasonable. Section 3 conferred upon the governor or the central government the power to declare an area as 'disturbed' without any independent review, oversight or scrutiny. The court did not see anything especially problematic with this power, with the exception that it now added the requirement that these declarations be reviewed (by the government itself) every six months. This periodic review, in the court's view, was a sufficient safeguard against declarations of 'disturbed areas' continuing indefinitely or for an extended period of time. Given that many regions had been declared 'disturbed areas' and had remained so for decades at the time of its decision, the court ought to have been more sceptical of arriving at this conclusion.

The 'licence to kill' section was upheld on the basis that it had inbuilt safeguards. The court did not think much of the issue that two of those safeguards were left entirely to the judgement of the relevant officer. It was for the officer to determine whether it was necessary to take action and also whether it was necessary to issue any warning at all before taking that action. It also declined to adopt the suggestion that the use of force under the AFSPA only be permitted against people that were armed. Leaving the 'licence to kill' section intact meant that unarmed violators of curfew orders could continue to be 'shot off hand'.[21]

On the 'licence to destroy', the court was told that the power was framed very broadly, as it enabled the destruction of any structures used as a hideout by armed gangs or absconders. This would apply equally to bunkers as it would to schools and hospitals. The court saw no merit in the argument, stating that this power was directed towards tracking down those who were evading legal process. The constitutional challenges to the 'licence to arrest' and the 'licence to search' sections were dismissed just as easily. These powers were not very different from the powers conferred upon police officers under the ordinary law, the court said. Section 6 of the AFSPA, which granted immunity from prosecution to officers without permission from the central government, was also upheld. For the court, this section did not grant impunity, but only granted the protection that officers needed to conduct their operations.

The army headquarters periodically circulated a memorandum entitled 'Dos and don'ts while acting under the Armed Forces (Special Powers) Act 1958'. The 'dos' in the list included acting in close communication with the civil administration, aiming 'low and short' when opening fire, and submitting a report to the police when handing over individuals that are arrested. Directions not to use excessive force, not to engage in torture and not to accept 'presents, donations and rewards' were all in the 'don'ts' section of the memorandum. The attorney general submitted this memorandum to the court, with a view to convincing the court that there was an 'effective check' against any misuse or abuse of powers under the AFSPA.

The court was persuaded, and asked the government to update the memorandum based on its decision in this case and previous cases. The court ordered that the memorandum be treated as a set of 'binding instructions' that members of the armed forces are obliged to follow. The court directed that any violations of these instructions must be taken seriously, and action should be taken against errant officers. Despite the court's decision, investigations about violations of these instructions were not taken seriously, with any meaningful action being a pipe dream. In 2012, an association that filed a PIL in the Supreme Court alleged that no action was taken against any officer in respect of over 1,500 unlawful killings by security officers in Manipur.

After over one and a half decades, the cases challenging the constitutional validity of the AFSPA were closed. The decision was seen as a resounding victory for the government, with the court's directions perceived as no more than token concessions (or as one eminent scholar put it, 'crumbs'[22]). The title of a story in the *Times of India* the day after the decision summarized it succinctly: 'Govt.'s power to deploy army in N-E upheld'.[23]

Two aspects of the Supreme Court's decision were particularly striking. First, the court's decision made virtually no reference to the fundamental rights to equality, freedom and life based on which the AFSPA was challenged,[24] or for that matter the legal tests to be applied to determine whether those rights had been violated. The court expended most of its intellectual capital on the issue of Parliament's competence to enact the AFSPA, without scrutinizing with any rigour whether it nevertheless violated fundamental rights. In some respects, the second issue was more important than the first, because it asked *whether* the law was constitutionally valid, rather than *who* could enact it. It is unclear if this happened because of the way in which the case was argued. In any event, it ought to have been obvious to the court that a section authorizing the use of *lethal force* should have been rigorously tested on the touchstone of *right to life* under Article 21 of the Constitution.

Second, the one benefit from the extended delay to the hearing of the case was that the court could consider how the AFSPA operated in practice over that period. However, despite the case being heard close to four decades after the AFSPA was enacted and fifteen years after some of the early petitions were filed, the Supreme Court's analysis focused on the language of the law without considering its lived realities. No constitutional analysis of a law that has been in force for a prolonged period can be complete without considering how that law operates on the ground. In this instance, the extensive evidence of human rights violations presented by the petitioners was put aside, with the question of constitutionality framed in very narrow terms.[25]

'Business as usual' resumed in the Northeast following the Supreme Court's decision. Most NGOs and human rights organizations reported that the list of 'dos and don'ts' – now judicially sanctioned – had little traction and was rarely observed in practice. In fact, reports by commissions of inquiry in the years after the court's decision revealed that there was little awareness of the list even among the armed forces. One report noted that senior officers in the armed forces were 'surprised' by some of the guidelines that were read out to them, while junior officers 'did not appear to have any idea' that a list of 'dos and don'ts' existed in the first place.[26] The fact that the court chose to dispose of the petitions following its ruling – rather than leave them pending to monitor compliance with its decision – made it especially challenging to hold successive governments to account.[27]

About three years after the court's decision, Irom Sharmila, then a twenty-eight-year-old Manipuri woman working with a human rights organization, commenced a hunger strike seeking the repeal of the AFSPA. She would be force-fed through a tube by the state for over sixteen years until she called off the strike at the age of forty-four, with her primary objective still unfulfilled. Aside from Sharmila's strike, the AFSPA survived a series of committees and commissions of inquiry that recommended its repeal. The Justice Jeevan Reddy Committee was established in 2005 to review the operation of the AFSPA after the killing of Thangjam Manorama in the custody of Assam Rifles. (Manorama was a thirty-two-year old Manipuri woman, alleged to be a separatist, who was brutally tortured and killed within hours of her arrest. This incident led to widespread protests across the state, including an iconic nude protest by twelve 'imas' [mothers] with banners reading 'Indian army rape us' and 'Indian army take our flesh'.) The committee observed that the AFSPA had become 'a symbol of oppression, an object of hate and an instrument of discrimination and highhandedness'.[28] It recommended repealing the AFSPA and placing some of its provisions into a different law, the Unlawful Activities (Prevention) Act of 1967.

The Second Administrative Reforms Commission of the central government, chaired by Veerappa Moily, also recommended the repeal of AFSPA in 2007.[29] In 2013, the Justice Verma Committee – chaired by the same judge who was on the bench that decided the Naga People's Movement case – stressed the need to review the continuance of the AFSPA 'as soon as possible'.[30]

The same year, the Justice Hegde Commission observed that the AFSPA had 'little or no effect' on insurgency in Manipur.[31] There was wisdom in this observation – something must have been amiss when 'disturbed area' notifications remained in place in the same location for decades.

From 2015 onwards, governments finally began lifting 'disturbed area' notifications from parts of the Northeast. By early 2019, disturbed area notifications were withdrawn entirely from Meghalaya, and from parts of Arunachal Pradesh and Tripura. The AFSPA itself, however, remains on the statute book despite its legitimacy having been chipped away for years by scholars, public officials and human rights organizations.[32] Unlike civil society organizations, the court had the authority to go beyond merely recommending, advising and warning. It missed the opportunity to do so in 1997. That error would prove especially costly.

10

Nandini Sundar

v

State of Chhattisgarh

Many of the chapters in this book demonstrate the impact and influence of judicial decision-making. Chief Justice M.C. Chagla's decision in the Narasu Appa Mali case during the Bombay monsoons in 1951 would result in religious 'personal laws' being immunized from the scrutiny of fundamental rights for decades. Chief Justice Y.V. Chandrachud's judgement in the Minerva Mills case in 1980 entrenched, once and for all, the position of the basic structure doctrine in India. And Justice S.R. Pandian's judgement in the Kartar Singh case in 1994 set the tone for continuing judicial deference to laws enacted in the name of national security. This chapter reveals the *limits* of the impact and influence of courts. A state-sanctioned armed civilian movement continued to thrive nearly a decade after being declared unconstitutional by the Supreme Court. A combination of political manoeuvring, adept litigation strategy and judicial delays have conspired to ensure that compliance with the court's judgement has been only in name.

~

Bastar, in the southern part of Chhattisgarh, was historically known for its dense forests and biodiversity. In recent decades, however, it has been at the epicentre of the Naxal movement in India. Since its emergence as a 'small but violent peasant insurrection'[1] in the 1960s, Naxalism has spread across the central 'forest belt' in several states, including West Bengal, Bihar, Odisha, Maharashtra, Madhya Pradesh, Jharkhand and Andhra Pradesh. However, no state has been as significantly affected as Chhattisgarh. The modus operandi of the movement ranged from sabotage of security forces and assassination of those with alternative viewpoints to attacks on state institutions and public services.

In this environment, Salwa Judum ('purification hunt' in Gondi, a language spoken by Adivasis in central India) was established as a counter-insurgency movement in

Chhattisgarh in 2005. Led by Congress leader Mahendra Karma, it was an armed civilian movement comprising thousands of Adivasis. The state maintained that Salwa Judum was a spontaneous uprising against the violence inflicted by the Naxalites. However, it was widely acknowledged as an 'officially sponsored civil war'[2] in which the state armed untrained Adivasis, many of them children, with weapons such as guns, axes, lathis, bows and arrows.

Salwa Judum had a thin veneer of legal sanction, as some of its members (including children) were appointed as 'special police officers' (SPOs) by the state. SPOs included not just some members of Salwa Judum, but also Adivasis, Dalits and some former Naxalites who had switched loyalties. As the name suggests, SPOs are meant to be appointed in special situations to tackle unlawful assemblies, riots or disturbances that the ordinary police is unable to contain on its own strength. They have the same powers, and are subject to the same duties, as ordinary police officers. The law contemplated that they be appointed to handle temporary situations, not long-term insurgencies.

Salwa Judum developed an ignominious reputation in a short span of time. Entire villages in Naxal-affected regions were burnt to the ground by the militia, with their residents shifted to 'relief camps'. Adivasis who were thought to sympathize with the Naxals were presumed guilty and killed without a semblance of due process. Incidents of rape were not uncommon. A newspaper report published less than a year after Salwa Judum's formation quoted Mahendra Karma as observing: 'Unless you cut off the source of disease, the disease will remain ... The source is the people, the villagers.'[3]

This disquieting state of affairs prompted a PIL in the Supreme Court in May 2007. The PIL was filed by Nandini Sundar, Ramachandra Guha and E.A.S. Sarma. Sundar was a professor of sociology at the Delhi School of Economics and had undertaken extensive research on Bastar. Guha was a prominent historian and author of several acclaimed books. Sarma was a former civil servant and previously commissioner for tribal welfare in the government of Andhra Pradesh. The PIL relied on four fact-finding reports by civil society organizations on the situation in Chhattisgarh. As members of the Independent Citizens' Initiative, Sundar, Guha and Sarma were part of the fact-finding missions for one of these reports, entitled 'War in the Heart of India'. The report estimated the death toll caused by Salwa Judum to be between 500 and 1,000 people in one year alone.[4]

Sundar, Guha and Sarma claimed that the state of Chhattisgarh had violated the fundamental rights of its citizens in promoting Salwa Judum and recruiting

SPOs for counter-insurgency operations. They claimed that the state not only violated the right to life of the citizens who came into contact with Salwa Judum and SPOs, but also the right to life of SPOs themselves, who were untrained and unprepared for counter-insurgency operations. Among the remedies they requested from the court were a direction to the government not to support the activities of Salwa Judum, an independent inquiry into the human rights violations committed by its members, and an order of compensation to the victims of Salwa Judum violence on par with the compensation paid to victims of Naxalite atrocities.[5]

By the time the hearings at the Supreme Court commenced towards the end of 2007, both sides had mobilized substantial legal teams. Senior advocate Ashok Desai and well-known criminal lawyer Nitya Ramakrishnan represented Sundar, Guha and Sarma. The Chhattisgarh government had a legal team that included, at different stages, senior advocates Harish Salve and Mukul Rohatgi. The central government was also represented at the hearings by a battery of prominent senior advocates – although Solicitor General Gopal Subramanium's refusal to appear at one of the key hearings caused some consternation.[6] As is often the case with PILs, the court chose to retain the case on its roster and schedule hearings periodically, often after long gaps of time between hearings, as opposed to hearing the case in a single unbroken stretch.

At one of the early hearings in April 2008, the court directed the NHRC to investigate and examine the allegations of the parties. The NHRC was tasked with establishing an appropriate fact-finding committee that would report back to the court under sealed cover with its findings on the atrocities committed by Salwa Judum and the Naxalites. The committee appointed by the NHRC lacked a diversity of viewpoints and consisted of IPS officers from the NHRC's investigative unit. Human rights activists criticized the composition of the committee as it did not include Adivasis from the area or representatives of NGOs as members (or, for that matter, to accompany the committee on its site visits).[7]

Further controversy developed as the deadline for the NHRC committee to submit its report drew nearer. The NHRC was slated to submit its report to the court on Tuesday, 26 August 2008. That morning, the *Economic Times*, a daily newspaper, carried an article with the headline 'NHRC Gives Thumbs Up to Salwa Judum Movement'.[8] The report claimed that the fact-finding committee had concluded that 'there was nothing to suggest' that Salwa Judum was directly involved in atrocities in Chhattisgarh, 'barring a few stray cases of violence'.[9] The article also said that the committee had found 'no evidence' that the Chhattisgarh government supported or promoted the activities of Salwa Judum. When questioned by Nandini Sundar about the source of the report, the author of the article commented that he did not receive it directly from the NHRC. This prompted Sundar to speculate that he could only have received it from the state government or central government[10] – suggesting that the report had been impermissibly leaked by the committee at least a day before it was presented to the Supreme Court, and possibly even earlier.

The NHRC committee report was staunchly criticized by Sundar and other human rights activists. The problems with the report were manifold. First, the process and methods deployed by the committee in its investigations were questionable. The committee travelled 'in a convoy of ten four-wheel drives and an anti-mine tank, preceded by road clearing exercises'.[11] This modus operandi made it impossible for the Adivasi to come forward and speak truthfully to the committee. The committee therefore came across many 'deserted villages in which people had run away'.[12] Second, the committee made some outright errors in planning the investigation – in some instances, for example, visiting a village with the same name as the village they were meant to visit.[13] Third, the committee often accepted the police's version of events (which was invariably sympathetic to Salwa Judum) uncritically, compromising on its own mandate as a fact-finding body.

Despite these problems with the investigation undertaken by the committee, there were still some disturbing findings in the report, which the Supreme Court caught on to. In particular, the court was anxious about the statement in the report that in some cases, no FIRs had been lodged by the police following killings by Salwa Judum in the state. It therefore directed the government of Chhattisgarh to ensure that FIRs were filed in such cases, and that an inquiry by a magistrate be ordered as and when a corpse was located. The government was asked to file an 'action taken' report to confirm compliance with the court's directions. The committee had also made recommendations on how to address the human rights violations in Chhattisgarh. In respect of those recommendations, the chief justice told the advocate for the government of Chhattisgarh: '[i]t is very painful to read the report . . . Whatever is urgently required to be done, do it.'[14] At least as far as the Supreme Court was concerned, this was hardly a 'thumbs up' for Salwa Judum.

A few months later, it was brought to the court's attention that the state government was not complying in full with the NHRC recommendations – filing FIRs, initiating magisterial investigations of deaths and redressing human rights violations. It was also alleged that the state government was supplying arms to members of Salwa Judum – an allegation the government 'denied emphatically'.[15] By this stage – now close to three years since the PIL had been filed – it appeared that the Supreme Court was losing its patience in the face of allegations and counter-allegations. The state government informed the court that over 3,000 SPOs had been appointed by the Chhattisgarh government in addition to the members of the regular police force (it did not clarify how many of these were also members of Salwa Judum).[16] Later, the court asked the state government to submit a report to the court to demonstrate compliance with the recommendations of the NHRC committee.[17]

As the hearings continued, the court focused its attention on the rehabilitation of Adivasis who had been displaced by Salwa Judum's clearing operations of villages. In January 2011, it noted that twenty-three relief camps were still functioning in the Dantewada and Bijapur districts. The court therefore reminded the state government of its 'constitutional duty and obligation' to facilitate the return of the Adivasis to their villages.[18] All victims of conflict – whether caused by Naxalites or the government of Chhattisgarh – were to be compensated. Schools and hostels that were occupied by security forces were ordered to be vacated.[19]

From the time the case was filed in 2007 until mid-

2011, no less than nine different judges – sitting in panels with one or two of their colleagues – heard the case. One of them – Justice B. Sudarshan Reddy – received an anonymous letter suggesting that as a member of the People's Union for Civil Liberties (which had filed an application to be added as a party to this case), it would be a conflict of interest for him to hear the case. The lawyers on all sides confirmed that they had no objection to his continuing to hear the case.

At least twenty-six hearings were scheduled during that period. While the case was simply adjourned on many occasions when it was called for hearing, the court continued to express its dismay at the state of affairs in Chhattisgarh. In one hearing, the judges are reported to have observed that 'the state should not encourage the common man by arming them to fight Naxalites'.[20] In another hearing, it was remarked that if private citizens were permitted to kill fellow citizens, the state ought to be 'liable to be prosecuted as an abettor of murder'.[21] However, the court had exercised restraint and refrained from invoking the 'nuclear' option – declaring Salwa Judum unconstitutional, directing that it be disbanded and ending the role of SPOs in counter-insurgency operations.

That would change in July 2011, when the court pronounced judgement in this case. A panel of Justice

B. Sudarshan Reddy (who was slated to retire from office that week) and Justice S.S. Nijjar declared the establishment of Salwa Judum unconstitutional and ordered that it be disbanded immediately. It also directed an immediate end to the deployment of the SPOs in counter-insurgency operations. The state and central governments were censured for their conduct from the time of the filing of the PIL in 2005. The state government was criticized for making misleading statements about its progress in complying with the court's directions. The court expressed its 'deepest dismay' with the central government for abdicating its constitutional responsibility by arguing that law and order was a 'state subject' and that it had no role in determining how SPOs would be recruited, trained or deployed.[22]

The Supreme Court catalogued multiple violations of the constitutional rights of both the SPOs and the residents of Chhattisgarh with whom they came into contact. The fundamental right to equality was violated by subjecting SPOs to the same risks as paramilitary personnel, who were better educated and better trained to perform counter-insurgency operations. Since SPOs cost much less to the public exchequer than paramilitary personnel, in the court's eyes there was an economic calculus behind this and 'issues of finance' had 'overridden other considerations'.[23] The central and state governments' assertion that SPOs were a useful 'force multiplier' gained no sympathy.[24] Constitutional values simply did not permit unethical means, no matter how effective or economical, to be justified by the ends.

The fundamental right to life was violated because uneducated and poorly paid Adivasi youngsters could not be expected to understand the dangers they faced in the performance of their functions and exercise sound judgement in confronting those dangers. The court lamented that SPOs had become 'cannon fodder' in the forests of Chhattisgarh.[25] The state could not discharge its obligation of providing security to all citizens by placing one group of citizens in the line of fire. Moreover, arming untrained SPOs with firearms endangered the lives of the residents caught in the crossfire.

The Supreme Court concluded its decision with a number of orders to the government of Chhattisgarh and the central government. All efforts were to be made to recall firearms provided to SPOs. Former SPOs were to be protected from revenge attacks by Naxalites. In future, SPOs could only be appointed to assist in disaster relief efforts and to regulate traffic, not to combat insurgents. The state government was ordered not only to prevent the operation of Salwa Judum, but also to promptly and diligently prosecute its past criminal activities.

This was a courageous decision. Prime Minister

Manmohan Singh had in 2006 described Naxalism as the 'single biggest internal security challenge' that India had ever faced.[26] As some of the other chapters in this book demonstrate, Indian courts – much like their counterparts in other regions of the world – are often reticent when confronted with questions of national security. The court did not mince its words, and neither did the news headlines of the time: 'SC terms arming Salwa Judum "unconstitutional"',[27] 'Salwa Judum is illegal, says Supreme Court',[28] 'Salwa Judum is illegal, scrap it, says SC'.[29] With a BJP government in the state and the Congress-led United Progressive Alliance (UPA) government in Delhi, posturing over what the judgement represented and who was to be held politically accountable began immediately.

Equally significant as the court's decision, however, was its diagnosis of the socio-economic causes behind the state of affairs in Chhattisgarh. The first twenty-two paragraphs of its judgement condemned the policies of the state, which privileged the interests of the extractive mining industry over those of the Adivasis. This sense of disenchantment against the state fuelled social unrest and established an environment in which Naxalism was able to thrive. For the court, this case was symbolic of 'a yawning gap between the promise of principled exercise of power in a constitutional democracy, and the reality of the situation in Chhattisgarh'[30] caused by '[p]redatory forms of capitalism'.[31]

These observations – seen as going beyond the institutional competence of the Supreme Court – were not well received. An *Economic Times* editorial criticized the court for passing 'facile judgement on economic paradigms and development strategies' and offering 'legitimacy to populist rants' on neo-liberalism.[32] In an indirect reference to the court's judgement, Arun Jaitley (who would later become union finance minister) noted that it was not for the court to debate the merits of economic liberalization – the 'Supreme Court of India cannot have an economic philosophy'.[33]

Shortly after the court's decision, the UPA government at the centre as well as the BJP-led state government in Chhattisgarh began exploring options to overturn the decision. The central government's primary concern was the knock-on effect that the decision would have on SPOs appointed in other states. Although Chhattisgarh was the only state represented at the hearing, there were passages from the decision that could be read as applying to SPOs across the country.[34] More than 50,000 SPOs were employed in various states aside from Chhattisgarh at the time – with over 30,000 in Jammu and Kashmir alone, and the balance spread across Odisha, Jharkhand, Andhra Pradesh, Maharashtra, Uttar Pradesh and Bihar.[35]

When asked about how it would respond to the decision, the minister of state for home affairs first noted in the Rajya Sabha that the central government was discussing the matter in consultation with the law ministry.[36] Following a few rounds of discussion with Attorney General Goolam Vahanvati, the plan that was originally envisaged was to file a petition seeking a review of the court's decision. However, thereafter the central government instead chose to file an application seeking a clarification on the scope of the decision. That application proved successful, with the Supreme Court clarifying that its decision was restricted to Chhattisgarh.[37] The damage limitation exercise was complete, and the central government no longer needed to be concerned about the tentacles of the decision extending to other states with SPOs.

The state government's initial thinking was also to file a review petition seeking the court's reconsideration of the decision. Moreover, a temporary 'stay' on the enforcement of the decision would, for the government, assuage the concerns associated with disbanding Salwa Judum and discharging the SPOs immediately – 'we will be spared the need to immediately give the marching order to SPOs',[38] one senior official noted. Gradually, however, its strategy grew more sophisticated. Rather than proceeding with challenging and reviewing the

Supreme Court's decision, the state government chose to accept and sidestep it instead.

The Chhattisgarh government filed an affidavit claiming that it had disbanded Salwa Judum and no longer used SPOs in counter-insurgency operations. Strictly speaking, this was true – or at least clever enough to avoid the charge of open defiance of the court's decision. However, it was highly misleading. Shortly after the judgement, a law was enacted establishing a Chhattisgarh Auxiliary Armed Police Force, to 'aid and assist the security forces' in maintaining order and combating Naxal violence.[39] This sounded strikingly similar to what the SPOs did before the Supreme Court's decision. The SPOs were appointed as members of this new force with effect from the date of the court's decision. This meant that the SPOs effectively retained their jobs following the decision. The state government's public justification for this new force was that its members were better paid, better trained and better equipped than SPOs – all of which was true, but which ignored the spirit of the court's concern with establishing a parallel force to undertake combat operations otherwise assigned to paramilitary forces. As Sundar said in an interview, 'The state government simply renamed the SPOs as Armed Auxiliary Forces with effect from the date of the judgement and gave them better guns.'[40]

Sundar, Guha and Sarma were alive to the state government's attempt to sidestep the decision. They filed contempt petitions in the Supreme Court, claiming the state government had complied with the decision only in name. This set off a cat-and-mouse game in which while the contempt petition awaited a full hearing, Salwa Judum regularly changed form over the years. The various avatars assumed by Salwa Judum since the Supreme Court's decision included the Jan Jagran Abhiyan, Vikas Sangharsh Samiti, Samajik Ekta Manch and Nagrik Ekta Manch.[41] All the while, the Supreme Court failed to implement the spirit of its decision, while the state government continued to proclaim formal compliance.

It is hard to diagnose the reasons for the colossal failure to meaningfully implement the Supreme Court's decision. Some scholars have criticized the court for framing its decision too narrowly, by focusing too much on the education, training and remuneration of SPOs rather than the inherent unconstitutionality of establishing an armed civilian movement.[42] This criticism is somewhat harsh, as there was enough in the court's decision to suggest that its apprehensions were categorical rather than narrow. Take, for example, paragraph 75, where the court ordered the state government to take 'all appropriate measures to prevent the operation of any group ... that in any manner or form seek to take law into private hands'.[43] The court's greater failing, however, was to allow the contempt petitions to linger on even as Salwa Judum took on different avatars.

The state government, on the other hand, executed perfectly the strategy of minimalistic, formal compliance with the court's decision whilst acting against its substantive content. Civil society, and in particular the mainstream media, did not provide it anywhere near the kind of coverage that the most politically salient cases of the time – such as the 2G spectrum case and the Bhullar death penalty case – received.[44] More than ten years, seventy hearings and one significant decision later, the court struggled to keep pace with the shifting manifestations of Salwa Judum.

Postscript

Now that you have read through the stories of India's ten forgotten cases, I conclude this book with some final reflections. When I finished writing the book, the first question I asked myself was – surely these cases must be the exception rather than the norm? In some respects, they are. Not every challenge to national security legislation takes the Supreme Court eighteen years to decide, or is decided close to four decades after the legislation was enacted (as in the Naga People's Movement case). No constitutional crisis would have ensued had Keshav Singh simply apologized for his 'pesky pamphleteering' (as his co-pamphleteers did) and accepted a reprimand from the Uttar Pradesh Legislative Assembly. Had it not been for Nani Palkhivala's masterful litigation strategy, the Minerva Mills case may well have been just another unremarkable case about the nationalization of a business. And the Mathura and R.D. Bajaj cases were unique simply because most women in their positions would not have filed police complaints in the first place, let alone pursue them to their logical conclusion.

However, upon closer scrutiny, many of the cases considered in this book exhibit features that are unnervingly common to their genre. The Champakam Dorairajan case was among the first to set into motion the idea that reservations are an exception to (rather than a facet of) the right to equality. This ignited the 'reservation versus merit' debate that plays out over and over in courts' decisions. R.D. Bajaj and Mathura yielded different outcomes – one ended in a conviction for Gill, the other in acquittals for Tukaram and Ganpat. But both decisions rested on gender stereotypes that are more common in the decisions of the courts than you may have hoped or expected (recall the Punjab and Haryana High Court's observation that Bajaj was a 'symbol of modesty' and the Supreme Court's finding that it could not 'take the girl [Mathura] at her word'). Cases such as Kartar Singh and Naga People's Movement symbolize the courts' broader refusal to meaningfully scrutinize legislation when the establishment invokes national security. The courts have upheld the most draconian national security laws with remarkable consistency, ignoring the lived realities of those who have had to suffer the consequences of these laws in practice.

Hopefully, reading about each of these cases would have left you not only with something to remember, but also much to reflect on and question.

Notes

1. The Keshav Singh Case

1. Theodore Lewis Becker, *Political Trials*,1971, p. 34.
2. Roughly translated from its original Hindi title ('*Shri Narsingh Pandey ke Kale Karnamon ka Bhanda-Fod*').
3. Fifth Lok Sabha, Members Bioprofile, http://164.100.47.194/loksabha/writereaddata/biodata_1_12/2181.htm
4. Sunil Gupta, 'A Tribute to Shri Jagadish Swarup', 1989, 3 SCC (Jour) 17.
5. Shanti Bhushan, *Courting Destiny: A Memoir*, Penguin India, 2008, pp. 92–95.
6. *Kesavananda Bharati v State of Kerala* AIR 1973 SC 1461.
7. Bhushan, *Courting Destiny*, pp. 92–95.
8. H.M. Seervai, *Constitutional Law of India*, 4th edn, 2007, p. 2170.
9. T.R. Andhyarujina, 'Studying the U.S. Supreme Court's Working', 1994, 4 SCC (Jour) 1.

10. Motilal C. Setalvad, *My Life: Law and Other Things*, Universal Law Publishing, 2012, p. 534.
11. *In Re Article 143 of the Constitution* AIR 1965 SC 745 [44].
12. Ibid.
13. *R v Paty* [1704] 92 ER 232.
14. *Murray's case* (1750).
15. *Stockdale v Hansard* (1839) 9 Ad & E 1 (KB).
16. 'This work has assumed the status of a exposition of parliamentary practice; and so, we think it would be an exercise in futility to attempt to deal with this question otherwise than by reference to May.'
17. *In Re Article 143 of the Constitution* AIR 1965 SC 745 [227].
18. P.K. Tripathi, 'Mr Gajendragadkar and Constitutional Interpretation', 1966, *Journal of the Indian Law Institute*, pp. 479, 535.
19. *MSM Sharma v Shri Krishna Sinha* AIR 1959 SC 395.
20. Constitution (44th Amendment) Act, 1978.
21. Constituent Assembly Debates, vol. X, 16 October 1949.
22. Setalvad, *My Life: Law and Other Things*, p. 532.
23. *Keshav Singh v Speaker, Legislative Assembly* AIR 1965 All 349.

2. Minerva Mills v Union of India

1. Pratap Bhanu Mehta, 'India's Unlikely Democracy: The Rise of Judicial Sovereignty', 2007, *Journal of Democracy*, 18(2), p. 112.
2. T.R. Andhyarujina, *The Kesavananda Bharati Case: The*

Untold Story of Struggle for Supremacy by Supreme Court and Parliament, Universal Law Publishing, 2011, p. 88.

3. The Constitution (42nd Amendment) Act, 1976, Statement of Objects and Reasons.
4. Ibid., Section 55.
5. Ibid.
6. Anita Ray and Vanita Venkatsubbiah, 'Political Development and Constitutional Reform: Some Recent Trends', 1981, *Economic and Political Weekly*, 16(3), pp. 81, 83.
7. Subroto Bagchi, 'Imagining Nandan Nilekani', Firstpost, 12 March 2010, https://www.firstpost.com/business/biztech/imagining-nandan-nilekani-1876931.html
8. Granville Austin, *Working a Democratic Constitution*, Oxford India Paperbacks, 2013, p. 498.
9. William Borders, 'Civil Libertarian and Gandhi Foe to Be Indian Ambassador to U.S.', *New York Times*, 19 August 1977.
10. The Constitution (44th Amendment) Act, 1978.
11. Austin, *Working a Democratic Constitution*, p. 421.
12. Chintan Chandrachud, 'Constitutional Interpretation', in *The Oxford Handbook of the Indian Constitution*, edited by Sujit Choudhry, Madhav Khosla and Pratap Bhanu Mehta, Oxford University Press, 2016, p. 81.
13. Nani Palkhivala, *We, the People: India – The Largest Democracy*, UBS Publishers, 1984, p. 210.
14. Ibid.
15. Indu Bhan, *Legal Eagles: Stories of the Top Seven Indian Lawyers*, Penguin Random House India, 2015.
16. Austin, *Working a Democratic Constitution*, p. 499.

17. Ibid., p. 500.
18. *Minerva Mills v Union of India* (1980) 3 SCC 625 [31].
19. Austin, *Working a Democratic Constitution*, p. 507.
20. *Minerva Mills v Union of India* (1980) 3 SCC 625 [84].
21. Ibid. [80]. While this is the figure cited in the Minerva Mills case, other sources have slightly different figures. Each of them is well over sixty days.
22. *Minerva Mills v Union of India* (1980) 2 SCC 591 [3].
23. Ibid. [4].
24. *Minerva Mills v Union of India* AIR 1980 SC 1789 [79].
25. Andhyarujina, *The Kesavananda Bharati Case*, p. 88.
26. Upendra Baxi, *Courage, Craft and Contention: The Indian Supreme Court in the Eighties*, N.M. Tripathi, 1985.
27. See Chandrachud, 'Constitutional Interpretation'.
28. *Minerva Mills & Others v Union of India and Others* AIR 1986 SC 2030.
29. *Minerva Mills v Union of India* (1980) 3 SCC 625 [78].
30. Abhinav Chandrachud, *Supreme Whispers: Conversations With Judges of the Supreme Court of India 1980–89*, Penguin Random House India, 2018.
31. *Kesavananda Bharati v State of Kerala* AIR 1973 SC 1461 [2219].
32. *Minerva Mills v Union of India* (1980) 3 SCC 625 [112].
33. Austin, *Working a Democratic Constitution*, p. 502.
34. *S.P. Gupta v Union of India* (1981) Supp SCC 87.
35. Salman Khurshid and Sudershan K. Misra, 'Supreme Court: A Bench Divided', *India Today*, 15 February 1981; Ashok Desai, 'Causes for Delay in the Supreme Court', *Times of India*, 2 April 1982.

36. 'Govt. to Pursue Review Petition', *Times of India*, 29 September 1980.

37. 'Law Minister's Attack on Supreme Court', *Times of India*, 30 November 1980.

38. 'Review to Be Sought: Parliament's Powers', *Times of India*, 12 August 1980.

39. Article 211 of the Indian Constitution.

40. Rajya Sabha Debates, 11 August 1980.

41. 'Powers: "No Need for Referendum"', *Times of India*, 12 August 1980.

42. Inder Malhotra, 'Changing the Constitution: Some Significant Stirrings', *Times of India*, 24 May 1984.

43. 'Powers: "No Need for Referendum"'.

44. N.A. Palkhivala, 'This Is Not the Time . . .', *Times of India*, 3 May 1981.

45. 'Reject Delhi Plea, Says Palkhivala', *Times of India*, 11 September 1980.

46. *Sanjeev Coke Mfg. Co. v Bharat Coking Coal Ltd.* (1983) 1 SCC 147 [10].

47. See Chintan Chandrachud, 'Constitutional Falsehoods', in *An Unconstitutional Constitution? Unamendability in Constitutional Democracies*, edited by Richard Albert and Bertil Emrah Oder, Springer, 2017.

3. Rameshwar Prasad v Union of India

1. Krishna K. Tumalla, 'Developments in Indian Federalism: 2005–2007', *Asian Journal of Political Science*, 15(2), pp. 139, 148.

2. Rediff.com, 'LJP Moves to Quell Rebellion', 22 May 2005.

3. *Rameshwar Prasad v Union of India* AIR 2006 SC 980 [10].

4. S.M. Khan, *The People's President: Dr A.P.J. Abdul Kalam*, Bloomsbury, 2016, chapter 4.

5. T.R. Ramachandran, 'Bihar Assembly Dissolved: Nitish Pre-empted; NDA Cries Foul, *Tribune*, 23 May 2005.

6. Purnima S. Tripathi, 'A Dissolution at Midnight', *Frontline*, 4–17 June 2005.

7. A.P.J. Abdul Kalam, *Turning Points: A Journey through Challenges*, HarperCollins, 2012, p. 172.

8. Times News Network, 'Cryptic Words Draw Out Bihar Suspense', *Times of India*, 30 September 2005.

9. Bishwajit Bhattacharyya, 'Conviction Yes, Sentence No: Why the SC's Bihar Judgment Is Stillborn', *Times of India*, 12 October 2005.

10. Times News Network, 'UPA Jolted as SC Strikes Down Bihar Dissolution: Polls to Go On, Govt May Make Buta Scapegoat', *Times of India*, 8 October 2005.

11. V. Ramakrishnan, 'A Verdict and the Vote', *Frontline*, 22 October–4 November 2005.

12. Tumalla, 'Developments in Indian Federalism, pp. 139, 148.

13. Ibid. [134].

14. Ibid. [145].

15. Ibid. [221].

16. Priya Singhal, 'SC Indicts Buta Singh', *India Today*, 6 February 2006.

17. Tumalla, 'Developments in Indian Federalism, 139, 149.

18. Khan, *The People's President*, chapter 4.

19. Kalam, *Turning Points*, p. 173.

4. Tukaram v State of Maharashtra

1. Moni Basu, 'The Girl Whose Rape Changed a Country', CNN, 8 November 2013.
2. *Tukaram v State of Maharashtra* (1979) 2 SCC 143.
3. Flavia Agnes, 'Law, Ideology and Female Sexuality: Gender Neutrality in Rape Law', 2002, *Economic and Political Weekly*, 37(9), p. 844.
4. *Tukaram v State of Maharashtra* (1979) 2 SCC 143.
5. Ibid.
6. *Maneka Gandhi v Union of India* AIR 1978 SC 597.
7. *Madhav Hayawadanrao Hoskot v State of Maharashtra* (1978) 3 SCC 544.
8. Upendra Baxi, Vasudha Dhagamwar, Raghunath Kelkar and Lotika Sarkar, 'An Open Letter to the Chief Justice of India', 16 September 1979, https://pldindia.org/wp-content/uploads/2013/03/Open-Letter-to-CJI-in-the-Mathura-Rape-Case.pdf
9. Ibid.
10. Mira Savara, 'Stirrings against Oppression', 1980, *Economic and Political Weekly*, 15(13).
11. Ibid.
12. Ibid.
13. Ibid.
14. 'Ten Years After', *Economic and Political Weekly*, 25(10).
15. Quoted in Savara, 'Stirrings against Oppression'.
16. Memorandum from Joint Action Committee Against Rape and Sexual Harassment, New Delhi (1980).
17. Mrinal Satish, *Discretion, Discrimination and the Rule of Law:*

Reforming Rape Sentencing in India, Oxford University Press, 2016, p. 40.

18. *Bharwada Bhoginbhai Hirjibhai v State of Gujarat* (1983) 3 SCC 217, 224.

19. Ibid.

20. Letter from P.B. Venkatasubramanian (Secretary, Department of Legal Affairs) to P.M. Bakshi (Member-Secretary, Law Commission of India), Appendix I to the Eighty-Fourth Report on Rape and Allied Offences: Some Questions of Substantive Law, Procedure and Evidence of the Law Commission of India, 1980.

21. Ibid.

22. Ibid.

23. The government referred the matter to the Law Commission on 27 March 1980. The Law Commission submitted its report on 25 April 1980.

24. Pratiksha Baxi, 'Rape, Retribution, State', 2000, *Economic and Political Weekly*, 35(14), p. 1196.

25. Ibid., p. 1197.

26. Ibid.

27. Upendra Baxi, 'Taking Suffering Seriously: Social Action Litigation in the Supreme Court of India', 1985, *Third World Legal Studies*, 4(6), p. 107.

5. R.D. Bajaj v K.P.S. Gill

1. Vipul Mudgal, 'Indecent Behaviour and Assault Land Punjab Police Chief K.P.S. Gill in Trouble', *India Today*, 31 August 1988.

Notes

2. Gayatri Rajwade, 'An Arduous Journey but Worth the Fight', *Tribune* (Chandigarh), 27 July 2005.
3. Ahsan I. Butt, *Secession and Security: Explaining State Strategy Against Separatists*, Cornell University Press, 2017, p. 107.
4. *R.D. Bajaj v K.P.S. Gill* AIR 1996 SC 309 [10–11].
5. Ibid.
6. Ibid.
7. *K.P.S. Gill v The State* MANU/PH/1180/1998 [10].
8. Correspondent, 'V.P. Singh Locks Horn with Punjab's New Governor Nirmal Mukarji over Chief Secretary Ojha', *India Today*, 15 February 1990.
9. C.S. Dogra, 'A Retired IAS Officer on How the #MeToo Movement Can Use Her Case Against K.P.S. Gill', Wire, 15 October 2018.
10. Times News Network, 'Julio Ribeiro on K.P.S. Gill', *Times of India*, 29 December 2001.
11. Ramesh Vinayak, 'Conviction of Supercop K.P.S. Gill Turns Spotlight on Sexual-Harassment Offences', *India Today*, 31 August 1996.
12. This was Akhil Gautam. See Rajwade, 'An Arduous Journey but Worth the Fight'.
13. Dogra, 'A Retired IAS Officer on How the #MeToo Movement Can Use Her Case Against K.P.S. Gill'.
14. Kalpana Kannabiran, 'Gendering Justice', 1996, *Economic and Political Weekly*, 31(33), p. 2223.
15. *State of Punjab v B.R. Bajaj* MANU/PH/0982/1989 [2].
16. Justice Shiv Charan Dass Bajaj.
17. *K.P.S. Gill v R.D. Bajaj* MANU/PH/0978/1989 [12].
18. Ibid. [6].

19. Ibid. [8].
20. Ibid.
21. Bhavdeep Kang, 'Brought Down a Peg', *Outlook*, 25 October 1995.
22. *R.D. Bajaj v K.P.S. Gill* AIR 1996 SC 309 [32].
23. Ibid. [23].
24. Ibid. [15].
25. Ibid. [17].
26. *R.D. Bajaj v K.P.S. Gill* AIR 1996 SC 309 [21].
27. Kang, 'Brought Down a Peg'.
28. Ibid.
29. Interview of Tavleen Singh, 'Taking Bottom-Slapping to Court Is Farcical', *Outlook*, 20 December 1995.
30. Reporter, 'R.D. Bajaj Interview to the BBC', BBC, 4 January 2017.
31. Vinayak, 'Conviction of Supercop K.P.S. Gill Turns Spotlight on Sexual-Harassment Offences'.
32. Ibid.
33. Cited in Kannabiran, 'Gendering Justice', pp. 2223–2224.
34. Ibid.
35. Ibid.
36. *K.P.S. Gill v The State* MANU/PH/1180/1998 [2].
37. Susan Abraham, 'Gill v/s Bajaj Judgment: Sentence Upheld, Conviction Withheld', 1998, *Lawyers Collective Journal*, 13(1), p. 24.
38. Ibid.
39. 'Gill's Conviction Upheld', *Frontline*, 24 January–6 February 1998.

40. *K.P.S. Gill v The State* MANU/PH/1180/1998 [61].
41. Ibid. [23].
42. Ibid. [28].
43. Ibid.
44. Ibid.
45. Ibid. [46].
46. Ibid. [54].
47. Rajwade, 'An Arduous Journey but Worth the Fight'.
48. Martha Nussbaum, 'The Modesty of Mrs Bajaj', in *Directions in Sexual Harassment Law*, edited by Catharine A. MacKinnon and Reva B. Siegel, Yale University Press, 2003, p. 635.
49. Rajwade, 'An Arduous Journey but Worth the Fight'.
50. Nussbaum, 'The Modesty of Mrs Bajaj', pp. 645–646.

6. State of Madras v Champakam Dorairajan

1. D. Kapur and P.B. Mehta, 'Mortgaging the Future? Indian Higher Education', *Indian Policy Forum* 159, 2007.
2. S. Vishwanathan, 'Proven Success', *Frontline*, April 2007.
3. Staff Reporter, 'Justice Party, Pioneer of Reforms, Turns 100', *The Hindu*, 25 November 2016.
4. Kalpana Kannabiran, *Tools of Justice: Non-Discrimination and the Indian Constitution*, Routledge, 2012, p. 168.
5. Y.M. Marican, 'The Genesis of the DMK', 1971, *Asian Studies* 340, 9(3), p. 352. The Congress party's refusal to accept the 'principle of communal representation' led to the resignation of the prominent leader E.V. Ramasamy 'Periyar'.
6. Vishwanathan, 'Proven Success'.
7. Austin, *Working in a Democratic Constitution*, p. 95.

8. *Champakam Dorairajan v State of Madras* AIR 1951 Mad 120 [1].

9. Mohan Parasaran, 'Legal Personalities and Their Role in Promoting Carnatic Music – Part 1', www.carnatica.net/special/legal1.htm

10. V.S. Ravi, 'Legal Luminary', *The Hindu*, 28 September 2003.

11. Article 37 of the Indian Constitution.

12. *Champakam Dorairajan v State of Madras* AIR 1951 Mad 120 [15].

13. Ibid.

14. Ibid. [35].

15. Ibid. [60].

16. Legal Correspondent, 'Invalidation of Communal GO: Madras Govt. to Appeal', *Times of India* (New Delhi), 11 August 1950, p. 7.

17. Austin, *Working in a Democratic Constitution*, p. 94.

18. Legal Correspondent, 'Communal G.O. Not Constitutional: Madras Case in Supreme Court', *Times of India* (New Delhi), 27 March 1951.

19. *State of Madras v Champakam Dorairajan* AIR 1951 SC 226 [10].

20. Ibid. [6].

21. Kannabiran, *Tools of Justice*, p. 171.

22. Ibid.

23. S.S.R. Reddy, 'Fundamentalness of Fundamental Rights and Directive Principles in the Indian Constitution', 1980, *Journal of the Indian Law Institute*, 22(3), p. 406.

24. Legal Correspondent, 'Communal G.O. Not Constitutional'.

25. Austin, *Working in a Democratic Constitution*, p. 97.

26. Ibid.

27. Arudra Burra, 'Freedom of Speech in the Early Constitution: A Study of the Constitution (First Amendment) Bill', in *The Indian Constituent Assembly: Deliberations on Democracy*, edited by Udit Bhatia, Routledge, 2017, p. 134.

28. V. Venkatesan, 'A Response in an Earlier Era', *Frontline*, September 2005.

29. Special Correspondent, 'Amendment Bill Referred to Select Committee, More Members to Serve on Body: Dr. Ambedkar Defends Measure in Parliament', *Times of India* (New Delhi), 19 May 1951.

30. Austin, *Working in a Democratic Constitution*, p. 97.

31. 'Communal G.O. Is Salvaged', 1951, *Economic and Political Weekly*, 3(3).

32. Vinay Sitapati, 'Reservations', in *The Oxford Handbook of the Indian Constitution*, edited by Sujit Choudhry, Madhav Khosla and Pratap Bhanu Mehta, Oxford University Press, 2016, p. 727.

33. P.K. Tripathi, *Spotlights on Constitutional Interpretation*, N.M. Tripathi, 1972, p. vii.

7. State of Bombay v Narasu Appa Mali

1. See Jayanth K. Krishnan, 'Legitimacy of Courts and the Dilemma of Their Proliferation: The Significance of Judicial Power in India', in *Asian Courts in Context*, edited by Jiunn-rong Yeh and Wen-Chen Chang, Cambridge University Press, 2015, p. 290.

2. Ibid., p. 291.

Notes

3. Sandra den Otter, 'Law, Authority and Colonial Rule', in *India and the British Empire*, edited by Douglas M. Peers and Nandini Gooptu, p. 169.
4. Abhinav Chandrachud, 'My Dear Chagla', *Frontline*, 7 September 2014.
5. *State of Bombay v Narasu Appa Mali* AIR 1952 Bom 84 [7].
6. Section 494, Indian Penal Code 1860.
7. *State of Bombay v Narasu Appa Mali* AIR 1952 Bom 84 [12].
8. Catharine A. MacKinnon, 'Sex Equality Under the Constitution of India: Problems, Prospects, and Personal Laws', 2006, *International Journal of Constitutional Law* 4, pp. 181, 197.
9. *State of Bombay v Narasu Appa Mali* AIR 1952 Bom 84 [6].
10. Ibid. [22].
11. Ibid. [10].
12. Indira Jaising, 'Gender Justice and the Supreme Court', in *Supreme But Not Infallible: Essays in Honour of the Supreme Court of India*, edited by B.N. Kirpal, Ashok Desai, et al., Oxford University Press, 2004, p. 298.
13. *Mohammed Ahmed Khan v Shah Bano Begum* AIR 1985 SC 945.
14. Flavia Agnes, 'Personal Laws', in *The Oxford Handbook of the Indian Constitution*, edited by Sujit Choudhry, Madhav Khosla and Pratap Bhanu Mehta, Oxford University Press, 2016, p. 914.
15. Ibid.
16. *John Vallamattom v Union of India* (2003) 6 SCC 611.
17. Indira Jaising, 'The Ghost of Narasu Appa Mali Is Stalking

the Supreme Court of India', *The Invisible Lawyer*, 1 September 2017.

18. *Shri Krishna Singh v Mathura Ahir* AIR 1980 SC 707 [15].

19. *Ahmedabad Women Action Group v Union of India* (1997) 3 SCC 573.

20. Chintan Chandrachud, 'Supreme Court's Lost Chance', *Indian Express*, 28 August 2017.

21. *Shayara Bano v Union of India* WP 118 of 2016 [22] (Justice R.F. Nariman).

22. *Indian Lawyers' Association v State of Kerala* WP (Civil) 373 of 2006, decided on 28 September 2018 [101] (Justice D.Y. Chandrachud).

23. *Masilamani Mudaliar and Others v The Idol of Swaminathaswaminathaswami Thirukoil* AIR 1996 SC 1697 (Justice Ramaswamy).

24. *Saumya Ann Thomas v Union of India* (2010) 1 KHC 811 [23].

25. Ibid. [22].

8. Kartar Singh v State of Punjab

1. *Liversidge v Anderson* (1941) UKHL 1.

2. *Korematsu v United States* (1944) 323 US 214.

3. *ADM Jabalpur v Shivkant Shukla* (1976) 2 SCC 521.

4. *Kartar Singh v State of Punjab* (1994) 3 SCC 569.

5. 'Black Law and White Lies – A Report on TADA', 1995, *Economic and Political Weekly*, 30 (18–19), p. 977.

6. Ujjwal Singh, 'Mapping Anti-terror Legal Regimes in India', in *Global Anti-Terrorism Law and Policy*, edited by Victor V.

Ramraj, Michael Hor, Kent Roach and George Williams, Cambridge University Press, 2005, p. 427.

7. Rajiv Wagh, 'Legal Experts Hope Indiscriminate Use of TADA Will End', *Times of India*, 5 August 1994.

8. Ibid.

9. Allwyn Fernandes, 'Cases Galore of TADA Misuse', *Times of India*, 28 September 1991.

10. Ibid.

11. Anil Kalhan, Gerald P. Conroy, Mamta Kaushal and Sam Scott Miller, 'Colonial Continuities: Human Rights, Terrorism, and Security Laws in India', 2006, *Columbia Journal of Asian Law*, 20 (93), p. 148.

12. Ibid., p. 147.

13. Molly Moore, 'India's Anti-Terror Law Draws Charges of Misuse; "Temporary" Act Jails 67,000 since 1985', *Washington Post*, 6 December 1994.

14. 'SC Refuses Relief to TADA Detenus', *Times of India*, 31 July 1992.

15. Rakesh Bhatnagar, '1,000 Writ Pleas against TADA', *Times of India*, 16 October 1991.

16. Ibid.

17. *Kartar Singh v State of Punjab* (1994) 3 SCC 569 [15].

18. Ibid. [22].

19. Ibid. [23].

20. Ibid. [251].

21. Ibid.

22. Ibid.

23. Ibid. [253].

24. Singh, 'Mapping Anti-terror Legal Regimes in India', p. 442.

25. For a fuller exposition of this argument, see Chintan Chandrachud, *Balanced Constitutionalism: Courts and Legislatures in India and the United Kingdom*, Oxford University Press, 2017, chapter 4.

26. *Kartar Singh v State of Punjab* (1994) 3 SCC 569 [295].

27. Ibid. [297].

28. Bisheshwar Mishra, 'SC Ruling Blunts TADA Stringency', *Times of India*, 13 March 1994.

29. K. Balagopal, 'In Defence of India: Supreme Court and Terrorism', 1994, *Economic and Political Weekly* 29, p. 2054.

30. Fali S. Nariman, 'Fifty Years of Human Rights Protection in India - The Record of 50 Years of Constitutional Practice', 2000, Student Advocate 12, pp. 4, 12.

31. 'Rights Panel for Review of TADA by SC', *Times of India*, 8 August 1994.

32. Moore, 'India's Anti-Terror Law Draws Charges of Misuse'.

9. Naga People's Movement of Human Rights v Union of India

1. Paul Banerjee, 'Communities, Gender and the Border: A Legal Narrative on India's North East', in *Challenging the Rule(s) of Law: Colonialism, Criminology and Human Rights in India*, edited by Kalpana Kannabiran and Ranbir Singh, SAGE, 2008.

2. Ibid.

3. The Armed Forces (Special Powers) Ordinance 1942; The Bengal Disturbed Areas (Special Power of Armed Forces)

Ordinance 1947; The Assam Disturbed Areas (Special Powers of Armed Forces) Ordinance 1947; The East Punjab and Delhi Disturbed Areas (Special Powers of Armed Forces) Ordinance 1947; The United Provinces Disturbed Areas (Special Powers of Armed Forces) Ordinance 1947; The Armed Forces (Special Powers) Act 1948.

4. Sanjib Baruah, 'AFSPA: Legacy of Colonial Constitutionalism', 2010, *Seminar* 615, https://www.india-seminar.com/2010/615/615_sanjib_baruah.htm

5. Constituent Assembly Debates, 11 December 1947, p. 1738.

6. A.G. Noorani, 'AFSPA: Urgency of Review', 2009, *Economic and Political Weekly*, 44 (34), p. 8.

7. Armed Forces Special Powers Act 1958, Section 5.

8. Sanjib Baruah, 'Routine Emergencies: India's Armed Forces Special Powers Act', in *Civil Wars in South Asia: State, Sovereignty, Development*, edited by Aparna Sundar and Nandini Sundar, SAGE, 2014.

9. Subir Bhaumik, 'India's Northeast: Nobody's People in No Man's Land', in *Internal Displacement in South Asia: The Relevance of the UN's Guiding Principles*, edited by Paula Banerjee, Sabyasachi Basu Ray Choudhary and Samir Kumar Das, SAGE, 2005, p. 164.

10. Staff Reporter, 'Indrajit Barua Passes Away', *Assam Tribune*, 28 June 2017.

11. Staff Reporter, 'Proceedings in Assam HC Stayed', *Times of India*, 12 May 1980.

12. Ibid.

13. Staff Reporter, 'Gauhati Petitions Transferred', *Times of India*, 10 June 1980.

Notes

14. *Naga People's Movement of Human Rights v Union of India* (1998) 2 SCC 109 [47].

15. Ibid. [48].

16. The Armed Forces (Punjab and Chandigarh) Special Powers Act 1983.

17. The Armed Forces (Jammu and Kashmir) Special Powers Act 1990.

18. Human Rights Watch, 'Getting Away with Murder: 50 Years of the Armed Forces (Special Powers) Act', August 2008.

19. National Human Rights Commission, *Annual Report 1995–1996*, p. 50.

20. Sudhir Krishnaswamy and Madhav Khosla, 'Military Power and the Constitution', *Seminar* 610, https://www.india-seminar.com/2010/611/611_sudhir_&_madhav.htm

21. A.G. Noorani, 'Supreme Court on Armed Forces Act', 1998, *Economic and Political Weekly*, 33(27), p. 1682.

22. Ibid.

23. Staff Reporter, 'Govt.'s Power to Deploy Army in N-E Upheld', *Times of India*, 28 November 1997.

24. See Noorani, 'AFSPA: Urgency of Review'.

25. Baruah, 'AFSPA: Legacy of Colonial Constitutionalism'; PUDR, 'An Illusion of Justice – Supreme Court Judgement on the Armed Forces (Special Powers) Act Report', http://www.unipune.ac.in/snc/cssh/HumanRights, p. 3.

26. Justice Santosh Hegde, *Report of the Supreme Court Appointed Commission*, 30 March 2013, para. 4.7.

27. Surabhi Chopra, 'National Security Laws in India: The Unravelling of Constitutional Constraints', *Oregon Review of International Law*, 17(1), p. 1.

28. Hegde, *Report of the Supreme Court Appointed Commission.*
29. *Fifth Report: Public Order, Second Administrative Reforms Commission Report*, 1 June 2007, p. 242.
30. Justice J.S. Verma, Justice Leila Seth, Gopal Subramanium, *Report of the Committee on Amendments to Criminal Law*, 23 January 2013, p. 151.
31. Hegde, *Report of the Supreme Court Appointed Commission*, p. 95.
32. The Punjab version of AFSPA was withdrawn in 1997, while the Kashmir version has continued in force.

10. Nandini Sundar v State of Chhattisgarh

1. Megha Bahree, 'The Forever War: Inside India's Maoist Conflict', 2010, *World Policy Journal* 27, pp. 83–84.
2. Nandini Sundar, 'Salwa Judum: Not a Path of Peace', *Economic Times*, 1 July 2006.
3. Somini Sengupta, 'In India, Maoist Guerrillas Widen "People's War"', *New York Times*, 13 April 2006.
4. Independent Citizens' Initiative, 'War in the Heart of India: An Enquiry into the Ground Situation in Dantewara District, Chhattisgarh', 20 July 2006, p. 27.
5. Nandini Sundar, 'Pleading for Justice', *Seminar*, 2010, p. 607.
6. Nistula Hebbar, et al., 'Why Did Subramaniam Skip Salwa Judum Hearing, Chidambaram Asks Law Ministry', 21 July 2011.
7. K. Balagopal, 'The NHRC on Salwa Judum: A Most Friendly Inquiry', *Economic and Political Weekly*, 43(51), p. 10.
8. Devesh Kumar, 'NHRC Gives Thumbs Up to Salwa Judum Movement', *Economic Times*, 26 August 2008.

9. Kumar, 'NHRC Gives Thumbs Up to Salwa Judum Movement'.
10. Nandini Sundar, 'Contempt of Court?', *Economic Times*, 28 August 2008.
11. Sundar, 'Pleading for Justice', p. 607.
12. Ibid.
13. Campaign for Peace & Justice in Chhattisgarh, 'Statement on NHRC Report on Salwa Judum', 19 October 2008.
14. 'Implement NHRC Recommendations on Salwa Judum, Supreme Court Asks Chhattisgarh Government', *The Hindu*, 20 September 2008.
15. *Nandini Sundar v State of Chhattisgarh* WP(Civil) 250 of 2007, Order of 18 February 2010.
16. Ibid.
17. Ibid., Order of 6 May 2010.
18. Ibid., Order of 18 January 2011.
19. Ibid.
20. 'Salwa Judum: SC Slams Govt for Arming Commoners', *Times of India*, 6 February 2009.
21. Dhananjay Mahapatra, 'Civilians Can't Be Armed to Fight Naxals', *Times of India*, 1 April 2008.
22. *Nandini Sundar v State of Chhattisgarh* AIR 2011 SC 2839 [41].
23. Ibid. [53].
24. Ibid. [33].
25. Ibid. [45].
26. 'India's Deadly Maoists', *Economist*, 26 July 2006.
27. 'SC Terms Arming Salwa Judum "Unconstitutional"', *Times of India*, 5 July 2011.

28. J. Venkatesan, 'Salwa Judum Is Illegal, Says Supreme Court', *The Hindu*, 5 July 2011.

29. Tanu Sharma, 'Salwa Judum Is Illegal, Scrap It, Says SC', *Indian Express*, 6 July 2011.

30. *Nandini Sundar v State of Chhattisgarh* AIR 2011 SC 2839 [1].

31. Ibid. [12].

32. 'Apex Court Ruling on Salwa Judum', *Economic Times*, 11 July 2011.

33. Atul Dev, 'Balancing Act: Chief Justice Khehar and the Tussle between the Executive and the Judiciary', *Caravan*, 1 June 2017.

34. This referred to paragraph 75(ii) of the court's decision, which read as follows: 'We order ... The Union of India to cease and desist, forthwith, from using any of its funds in supporting, directly or indirectly the recruitment of SPOs for the purposes of engaging in any form of counter-insurgency activities against Maoist/Naxalite groups ...'

35. 'Govt to Seek Salwa Judum Verdict Review', *Mint*, 4 August 2011.

36. Rajya Sabha Debates, 3 August 2011, Question 41.

37. *Nandini Sundar v State of Chhattisgarh* WP (Civil) 250 of 2007, Order of 18 November 2011.

38. 'Salwa Judum: Govt to File Review Petition against SC Order on SPOs', *Economic Times*, 9 July 2011.

39. The Chhattisgarh Auxiliary Armed Police Force Act 2011.

40. 'Chhattisgarh government has simply ignored Supreme Court's orders ... seems intent on replicating Salwa Judum', *Times of India*, 16 October 2015.

Notes

41. Nandini Sundar, 'Darkness at Noon in the "Liberated Zone" of Bastar', Wire, 4 February 2016.
42. See Vinay Sitapati, 'The Impact of the Indian Supreme Court', *India International Centre Quarterly*, 41(2), pp. 52, 59.
43. *Nandini Sundar v State of Chhattisgarh* AIR 2011 SC 2839 [75].
44. See Chintan Chandrachud, 'Measuring Constitutional Case Salience in the Indian Supreme Court', 2016, *Journal of Indian Law and Society* 6, p. 42.

Acknowledgements

I am grateful to Mrinali Komandur, Anant Sangal, John Simte and Ayushi Singhal for their outstanding research assistance. I would like to thank Sergio Guiliano (Italiano) for access to research resources and discussions on some of the chapters. I would also like to thank Parth Mehrotra for being a thoughtful editor and critic, and the Juggernaut team for their unwavering enthusiasm.

I would like to acknowledge those who have supported my family during difficult times. They are Dr Meena and Dr Praful Desai, Madhavi and Jay Desai, Meenakshi and Justice Girish Kulkarni, Sudha and Justice R.M. Lodha, Rajee and Justice S. Radhakrishnan, Anjana and Birendra Saraf, and Meeta and Dr Satyavan Sharma. I owe them an eternal debt.

Acknowledgements

Aai continues to inspire me every day. I am grateful to Dad, Kalpana, Abhinav, Ba, Papa, Mom and Dimple for their unconditional love, support and encouragement. My biggest thanks are to Disha, whose love sustains me.

1

CRAFTED
FOR MOBILE
READING

*Thought you would never read a book
on mobile? Let us prove you wrong.*

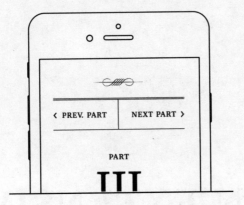

Beautiful Typography

The quality of print transferred
to your mobile. Forget ugly PDFs.

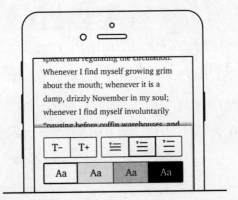

Customizable Reading

Read in the font size, spacing
and background of your liking.

AN EXTENSIVE LIBRARY

Including fresh, new, original Juggernaut books from the likes of Sunny Leone, Praveen Swami, Husain Haqqani, Umera Ahmed, Rujuta Diwekar and lots more. Plus, books from partner publishers and loads of free classics. Whichever genre you like, there's a book waiting for you.

DON'T
JUST READ;
INTERACT

We're changing the reading experience from passive to active.

juggernaut.in

Ask authors questions

Get all your answers from the horse's mouth.
Juggernaut authors actually reply to every
question they can.

Rate and review

Let everyone know of your favourite reads or
critique the finer points of a book – you will be
heard in a community of like-minded readers.

Gift books to friends

For a book-lover, there's no nicer gift than
a book personally picked. You can even
do it anonymously if you like.

Enjoy new book formats

Discover serials released in parts over
time, picture books including comics,
and story-bundles at discounted rates.
And coming soon, audiobooks.

juggernaut.in

4

LOWEST PRICES & ONE-TAP BUYING

Books start at ₹10 with regular discounts and free previews.

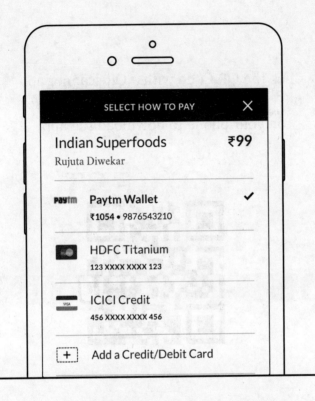

Paytm Wallet, Cards & Apple Payments

On Android, just add a Paytm Wallet once and buy any book with one tap. On iOS, pay with one tap with your iTunes-linked debit/credit card.

Click the QR Code with a QR scanner app
or type the link into the Internet browser
on your phone to download the app.

For our complete catalogue, visit www.juggernaut.in
To submit your book, send a synopsis and two
sample chapters to books@juggernaut.in
For all other queries, write to contact@juggernaut.in